Traditional Country Furniture

21 PROJECTS IN THE SHAKER, APPALACHIAN AND FARMHOUSE STYLES

FROM THE EDITORS OF POPULAR WOODWORKING

POPULAR WOODWORKING BOOKS

CINCINNATI, OHIO

www.popularwoodworking.com

Contents

Kentucky Sideboard 4

Spice Cabinet 12

Military Writing Desk...................... 22

Entertainment Center..................... 26

Franklin Chair 44

Drop-front Secretary....................... 54

Roadhouse Pipe Box 66

Country Dry Sink 68

Blanket Chest 74

Burlington Farmer's Desk............... 84

Wastebasket 88

4 Ways to Build A Tavern Table 98

Country Wall Shelf 106

Stepstool... 112

Drop-leaf Kitchen Table 120

Medicine Cabinet 128

Antiqued Tabletop Hutch.............. 132

Lamp Table 136

Corner Wall Cabinet....................... 150

Queen Anne Side Tables 162

Shaker Tall Clock 168

Resources 175

Kentucky Sideboard

Kentucky furniture is a style all its own,
marked by solid, honest construction with
a trace of whimsy in its ornamentation.

by Warren A. May

Warren A. May has been crafting solid-wood furniture and mountain dulcimers for more than 25 years. His showroom and dulcimer workshop is located at 110 Center St., on the College Square in Berea, the arts and crafts capital of Kentucky.

It's unlikely you'll find the "Kentucky Style" listed in any furniture-design textbook, but it's real. I've spent the last 15 years tracking down examples of this 18th- and 19th-century furniture style to study and incorporate elements of it into my own furniture pieces.

Kentucky furniture is less ornate than the pieces produced in the cities of its day, and this befits its frontier heritage. One of the things that sets Kentucky furniture off from other vernacular forms is the inlay that adorns the drawers and legs. While I've seen some examples of the Kentucky style with complex inlay designs, most times the inlay is simple and understated.

The furniture itself is usually made using walnut or cherry, two woods that are common in most parts of the Bluegrass state.

I've been building the sideboard design shown here for a number of years, and it has been received enthusiastically by my customers – no matter which side of the Mason-Dixon line they're from. A three-drawer version also is popular, and it is an easy change should you prefer that arrangement.

This sideboard is built using straightforward joinery and requires only 2"-square material for the legs. In deciding which inlay design to use, I pay careful attention to the wood grain, looking for the perfect flow of grain and contour. Just as with the authentic pieces of Kentucky-style furniture built in the 1700s and 1800s, I let hand-carved knobs and inlaid diamond escutcheons add a special flair.

I've made a simple mortising jig to help me locate the mortises in the sideboard legs. The jig is made from a piece of oriented strand board (OSB) and a couple of stop blocks screwed to the OSB that position the part to be mortised (above). A handscrew secures the leg against the stop block. I use a $\frac{3}{8}$" spiral bit and my router's template guide to rout the mortise in several passes (right).

cutting list

NO.	ITEM	DIMENSIONS (INCHES)		
		T	W	L
4	Legs	2	2	33⅛
2	Ends	⅞	13⅜	13¼
1	Back	⅞	13	42½
1	Top face frame rail*	⅞	2	43½
1	Bottom face frame rail*	⅞	4½	43½
1	Center face frame stile*	⅞	2	8
1	Top	⅞	18	48
1	Backsplash	⅞	5	46½
2	Drawer fronts	⅞	7	20¼
4	Drawer sides	½	7	16
2	Drawer backs	½	6⁷⁄₁₆	20¼
2	Drawer bottoms	5⁄16	15¾	19¾
1	Support frame front	⅞	2	44¾
2	Support frame ends	⅞	2	13½
1	Support frame center	⅞	4	13½
4	Drawer guides	½	½	15½
2	Drawer kickers	⅞	2	15½
1	Drawer support cleat	⅞	2	4
2	Mounting cleats	⅞	2	41
4	Drawer stops	¼	1	2

* Length includes ½" tenons on both ends.

Begin Construction

If you're interested in making your own version of this piece, I encourage you to try the inlay details. But if the sideboard itself is what you're after, I've offered the article in two sections. The main article shows you how to make the case, while the side-story explains the inlay work.

Start building the case by first marking the legs for the mortise-and-tenon joints in the face frame. These are the only mortise-and-tenon joints in the piece. The back and sides are held in place on the legs using biscuits.

To mark the mortise and tenon locations, measure down 2" from the top of each leg and mark for the top rail. Then measure another 7" down to define the drawer space and the location of the top of the lower rail. Go ahead and measure another 2½" and 4¼" from the drawer space. The 2½" mark is the

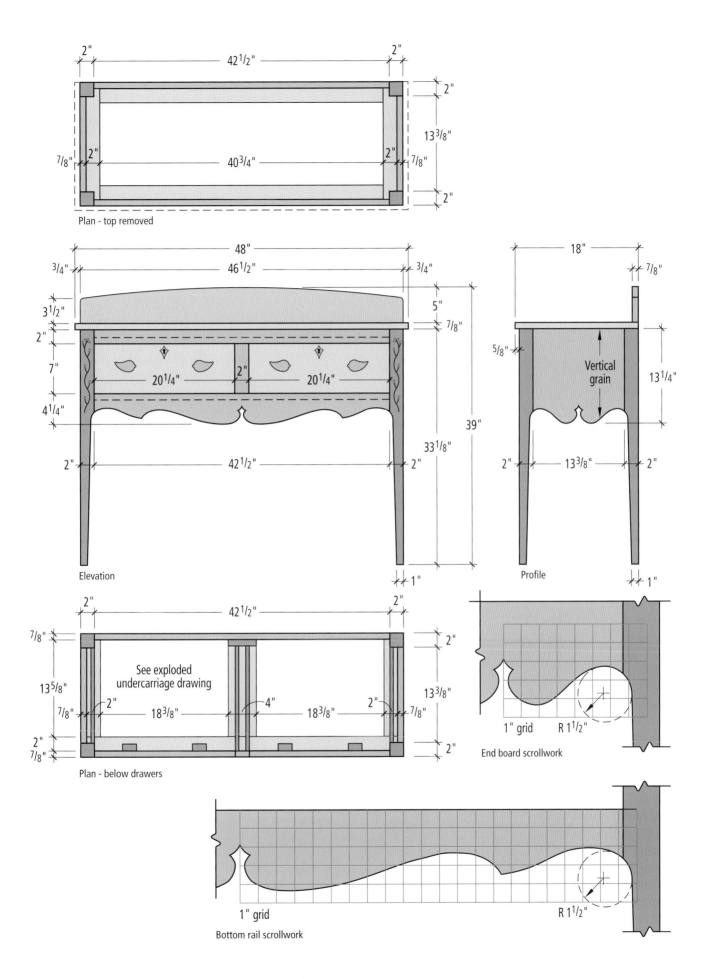

Plan - top removed

2" 42 1/2" 2"
2"
13 3/8"
7/8" 2" 40 3/4" 2" 7/8"
2"

Elevation

48"
3/4" 46 1/2" 3/4"
3 1/2"
2"
7"
4 1/4"
5"
7/8"
20 1/4" 2" 20 1/4"
2" 42 1/2" 2"
39"
33 1/8"
1"

Profile

18" 7/8"
Vertical grain
5/8"
13 1/4"
2" 13 3/8" 2"
1"

Plan - below drawers

2" 42 1/2" 2"
7/8" 2"
13 5/8"
See exploded undercarriage drawing
7/8" 2" 18 3/8" 4" 18 3/8" 2" 7/8"
2"
7/8"
2"
13 3/8"

End board scrollwork

1" grid R 1 1/2"

Bottom rail scrollwork

1" grid R 1 1/2"

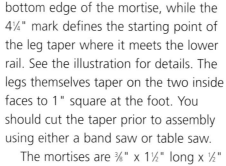

Drawer face
7/16" dowel
3/4" plug, bored
1/2" stock

Section

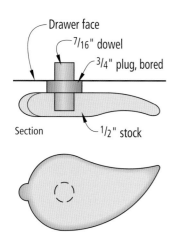

Half-scale pull details

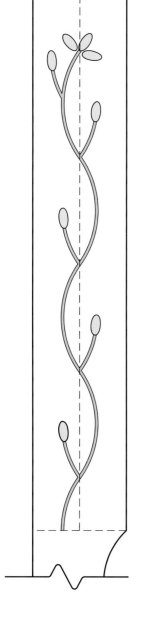

bottom edge of the mortise, while the 4¼" mark defines the starting point of the leg taper where it meets the lower rail. See the illustration for details. The legs themselves taper on the two inside faces to 1" square at the foot. You should cut the taper prior to assembly using either a band saw or table saw.

The mortises are ⅜" x 1½" long x ½" deep and positioned so the front frame pieces are flush to the front of the legs. When making the mortises, add an extra ¹⁄₁₆" to the depth to ensure the tenons' shoulders seat tight against the legs. Cut the mortises in the legs and in the rails, which are for the center face-frame stile.

Now cut the tenons on the two face-frame rails and center stile, and use the scaled diagrams to cut the scrollwork on the lower face-frame rail. Shape the transition from the rail to the leg.

If you're going to add inlay work to your sideboard, you should skip ahead to the section titled "Inlay, Kentucky Style" at this time and do the work on the legs prior to gluing up the carcase.

Now turn your attention to the two ends of the cabinet. The end panels are glued between the legs with the grain running vertically. With the panels glued up, crosscut the top edge to create a clean, straight line. Then mark on the ends where the legs should intersect – it's the same point where the scrollwork intersects the legs on the front.

Sketch the scrollwork pattern on the ends and cut it to shape on the band saw. Now glue the end panels between the legs, flush to the outside surface of the legs (this is a long-grain joint, but you can use biscuits to help align everything), and let things dry while you work on the back.

The back is a solid panel with the grain running horizontally and is bis-

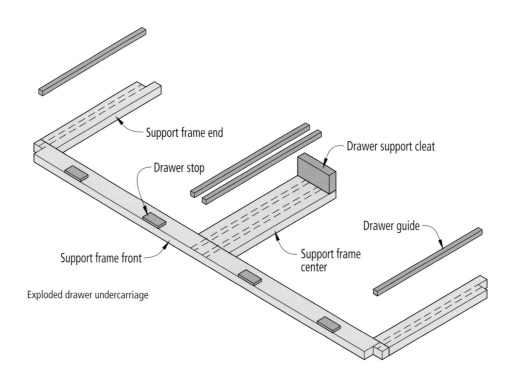

Support frame end

Drawer support cleat

Drawer stop

Drawer guide

Support frame front

Support frame center

Exploded drawer undercarriage

After shaping the pattern on the bottom edge of the two ends, they can be glued between the two legs. I used two pieces of scrap wood to protect the legs during glue-up, but I always end up a hand short during these operations. So I taped the scrap pieces to the legs to keep them in place, hands-free. After the end assembly is dry, I took advantage of the ability to still lay the end flat and used a chip-carving knife to soften the edges of the scroll-work by adding a slight bevel (right).

cuited between the back legs, again flush to the outside of the back legs. Cut a pattern on the back that is similar to the pattern on the bottom face-frame rail, but without the diamond-shaped cutout or the horns beneath the drawers.

With the end assemblies, back and front frame ready, sand all your case parts and then glue the front frame, end assemblies and back together. Measure diagonally from leg to leg to determine if the case is square.

Supporting the Drawers

The drawer support frame is next. Notch the support frame front between the front legs so it fits tight against the bottom face frame rail. Now notch the two support frame ends around the back legs. These pieces should fit between the front support rail and be just short of the back. Overall you want the frame to be ⅛" shy of the rear legs and back to allow for wood movement in the end pieces.

The drawer support frame is assembled and attached to the case using screws. First drill and ream out a few holes in the support frame ends. The sloppy

The support frame is screwed together after being notched to fit inside the assembled carcase. Remember to leave space for wood movement on the end pieces. Also, it's important for smooth drawer operation that the support frame pieces are flush on the top surface. I clamped a scrap piece carefully across the joint during assembly to make sure the frame remained flush.

holes allow for wood movement. Now drill several holes through the support frame front that allow you to attach it to the bottom face-frame rail. Now use screws to attach the front, ends and center support together as shown in the photo at right.

Glue and screw the support frame to the bottom face-frame rail, and screw the support frame ends to the end panels. Fasten the center support to the back with a cleat. The cleat is screwed to the back, above the center support, then screwed to the support, again using slotted holes to allow for movement.

Now notch and install the drawer kickers (which support the tops of the drawers). Attach these flush to the bottom edge of the top face-frame rail. Use the same method you used to attach the support frame end pieces.

Now is the ideal time to add the mounting cleats that attach the top to the case. Glue these cleats flush to the top of the case to the back and the top face-frame rail. Drill holes in the cleats and kickers so you can screw the top in place. Note that there's no need to ream out these holes to allow for wood movement. The case will expand and contract from front to back thanks to the vertical grain of the ends.

Before you attach the top, you should build the drawers. You need to screw in some drawer guides and stops, and that's easier to do with the top off.

Drawers

Matched drawer fronts are a nice touch for this cabinet. Select a board wide and long enough to yield both drawer fronts. The drawers are of classical construction, using half-blind dovetails on the front-to-sides joint, and through-dovetails at the back. I hand-cut my dovetails, but it's up to you how you proceed from here.

The drawer bottoms are solid $\frac{5}{16}$"-thick panels, fit into grooves cut ¼" up from the bottom of the drawer front and sides. The back is $\frac{9}{16}$" narrower than the sides, so the bottom can be slipped in from the rear, then attached to the drawer back. Once the drawers are built, screw in drawer runners to the support frame. Then screw ¼"-thick stops that keep the drawer fronts aligned with the front of the face frame.

With the drawers fit, it's time to get the top ready to attach. The top is a simple flat panel, glued up as necessary to make the needed width. It extends over

Once the carcase is assembled, add the top cleats and fit the drawer guides and stops. This is much easier to do without the top attached, so save that for the last.

the front edge of the carcase by $\frac{5}{8}$", and ¾" over each end and is held flush to the back.

Make a back splash the same length as the carcase, screwing and gluing the splash to the top. The splash can be a simple large arch, or you can add a design of your choosing. Attach the top by screwing it to the cabinet through the two drawer kickers and the two cleats glued in earlier.

Adding a Finish

To finish the piece I used an oil finish to start. I applied one coat of oil, then let that dry for five days. I then sprayed two coats of lacquer sanding sealer, sanding with 240-grit sandpaper between coats, then I added another two coats of semi-gloss lacquer, rubbing out the final coat with #0000 steel wool. As a last touch I wiped the entire piece down with a layer of spray wax.

Inlay, Kentucky-style

Now you have the basic information to create a simple, but attractive sideboard. By adding some inlay to the piece, it comes to life.

My trailing vine and bellflower inlays have been most challenging. Even with routers, chisels and a variety of modern tools it is still slow work, but it is worth the effort.

Try line inlay with an Xacto knife with two blades in it. Or you can also rout a groove. I made a simple following template with a gentle curve, then I use a Rotozip with an added base with a strip of slick stuff on the bottom - a small guide slightly larger than the ground bits makes it easy to follow a curve (photo top).

Next I cut a straight piece of rock maple in the table saw and rip it with a backing board on the band saw, slightly wider than the depth of the groove. I then glue the strip in place, using the head of my chisel to push the strip into place a section at a time. It usually looks better than you think it should (photo top right).

If you're a beginner, try simple leaves. I start by cutting football shapes from a contrasting wood with a sharp gouge. I then cut the recess with the same tool and glue the "leaves" or "petals" in place.

Another method is to cut a leaf, diamond or bellflower design in a 2"-thick piece of maple, then resaw the piece to the desired thickness on the band saw (photo right).

All of the inlays require a certain amount of hand-fitting. By leaving the inlay pieces proud of the surface, they're easier to handle, and I can complete the entire section before sanding everything flush. The bellflower has a second step. I use a torch to lightly burn the edges of the inlay to apply shading before gluing them in place in their recesses.

Don't be afraid to experiment, but you might want to make your first few attempts on test pieces rather than on a finished piece of furniture. You'll be surprised how easy it is.

Spice Cabinet

by Jim Stack

I designed this spice rack with visual movement in mind. Visual movement is an important consideration when designing furniture or cabinetry. The coves on the front and sides of the top and bottom parts of this spice cabinet guide your eye around the cabinet. Also, your eye will follow the angled doors to see where they go.

This cabinet is made of white pine, which was purchased at a local home-improvement center in the form of 1x10s that were 8' in length. The wider boards are more likely to have knot-free wood, or at least more wood that's clear and usable.

Originally, I was going to make door frames and install glass panels. Instead, I saw some honey-colored wood in one of the boards that just begged to be made into panels for the doors.

Basic woodworking skills are all that you need to make this cabinet. I used only a table saw and a router. I fit the doors with a hand plane after using the table saw to cut the bevels on the edges. After sanding the whole cabinet with 220-grit sandpaper, I finished the inside of the cabinet with thinned (about 400 percent) shellac. It will smell good every time the cabinet is opened. The outside of the cabinet was finished with two light coats of wipe-on polyurethane.

Full-scale section detail of cabinet back slats with shiplap joints

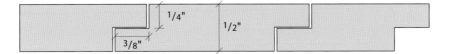

1/4"
1/2"
3/8"

Back slats are random widths.

Profile for top/bottom A

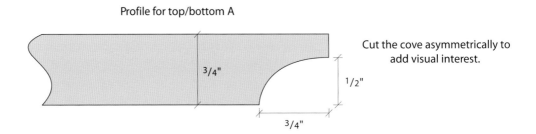

Cut the cove asymmetrically to add visual interest.

3/4"
1/2"
3/4"

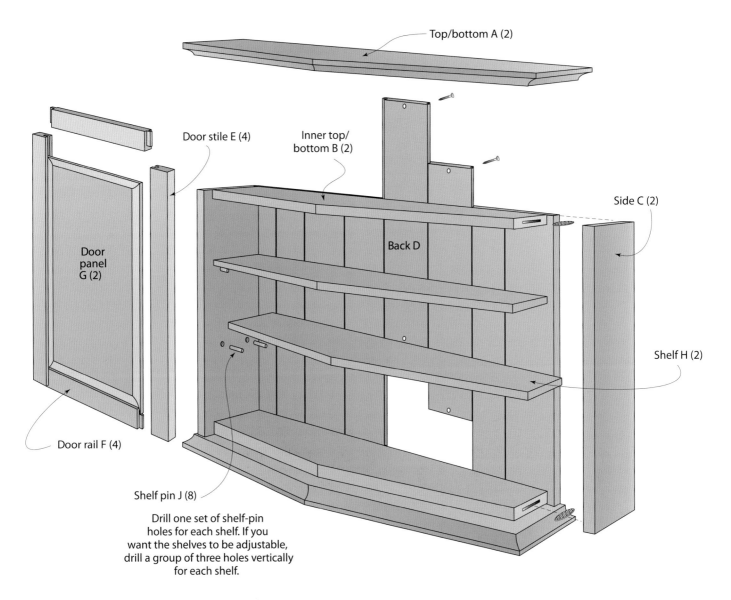

Top/bottom A (2)

Door stile E (4)

Inner top/
bottom B (2)

Side C (2)

Back D

Door
panel
G (2)

Shelf H (2)

Door rail F (4)

Shelf pin J (8)

Drill one set of shelf-pin
holes for each shelf. If you
want the shelves to be adjustable,
drill a group of three holes vertically
for each shelf.

cutting list

INCHES (MILLIMETERS)

REFERENCE	QUANTITY	PART	STOCK	THICKNESS	(mm)	WIDTH	(mm)	LENGTH	(mm)	COMMENTS
A	2	top/bottom	white pine	3/4	(19)	8	(203)	26	(660)	
B	2	inner top/bottom	white pine	5/8	(16)	5 3/4	(146)	22 1/2	(572)	
C	2	sides	white pine	3/4	(19)	5 1/4	(133)	16	(406)	
D	1	back	white pine	1/2	(13)	16	(406)	23 1/2	(597)	back is made of random width boards using shiplap joints
E	4	door stiles	white pine	3/4	(19)	1 1/2	(38)	15 7/8	(403)	
F	4	door rails	white pine	3/4	(19)	1 1/2	(38)	9 7/16	(240)	
G	2	door panels	white pine	1/2	(13)	9 3/16	(233)	13 3/4	(349)	
H	2	shelves	white pine	3/4	(19)	5 1/2	(140)	22 15/16	(583)	
J	8	shelf pins	hardwood dowel	1/4 dia.	(6)	3/4	(19)			

HARDWARE & SUPPLIES

4	No. 20 biscuits
20-25	1 1/4" (32mm) drywall screws
	wood glue
4	1 1/2" (38mm) butt hinges

STEP 1 Start this project by cutting out the top/bottom parts. Cut the parts to the width and length shown in the materials list. Then lay out the front angles. Temporarily join the two parts together with double-stick tape. Cut them using a jigsaw or band saw. Smooth the saw cuts using a hand plane or power jointer. Finally, draw the rest of the cabinet on the top. Cut out the inner top/bottom and the sides, using these lines as your guides for sizing the parts. This ensures they will all fit together properly.

STEP 2 Cut the 1/2" × 1/2" rabbets on the back edges of the sides using a dado stack set up in your table saw. You could also cut these rabbets with a single blade by first standing the parts on edge and making the first cut. Then lay the parts flat and make the second cut to remove the material to create the rabbet. If you use a dado stack, you'll need to attach a sacrificial fence to the table saw fence because the dado blades will cut slightly into the fence.

STEP 3 Use biscuits and glue to join the inner top/bottom to the sides.

STEP 4 When gluing the sides to the inner top/bottom parts, double-check the cabinet for squareness.

STEP 5 Cut enough boards to create the back of the cabinet. Using several individual boards to make the back rather than making it one solid piece minimizes the seasonal movement in the wood. Make the shiplap joints using the same dado setup you used in step 2. Then attach the back boards with a single 11/4" drywall screw in the center top and bottom of each one. Use no glue.

STEP 6 Cut the cove on the ends and front of the top/bottom parts, using a router. To give the cove more visual interest, cut it asymmetrically. (See the illustration for details.)

STEP 7 Glue the top/bottom parts to the cabinet.

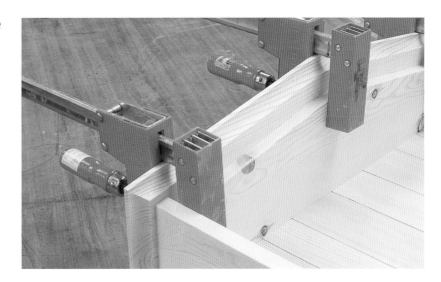

STEP 8 Cut out the door parts. Using a single blade, cut a 1/4"-wide by 3/4"-deep groove in the center of the stiles and rails. To center the groove, make the first cut slightly off center. Then flip the part end for end and make the second cut to create the groove.

STEP 9 Cut 1/4"-wide by 3/4"-long tenons on the rails by setting the fence to the length of the tenon. Nibble the wood with the saw blade, then flip the rail over to complete the tenon. This will automatically center the tenon on the rail. Fit the tenons first using some scrap wood.

STEP 10 Use the router to cut the cove on the door panels. You could also raise the panels by cutting a 12° bevel on the panel edges.

STEP 11 When assembling the doors, glue them up on a flat surface. Apply glue only on the frame joints. Let the panel float in the frame.

STEP 12 Make a router jig to cut the mortises for the door hinges. (See "Jig for Routing a Hinge Mortise" on the next page.) The depth of the mortise will dictate the spacing between the door and the cabinet side.

STEP 13 This is the bird's-eye view of the cut mortise. Use a chisel to square the corners of the mortise.

STEP 14 The hinge is installed with the barrel located proud from the door front. This allows the door to swing a full 180°. Cut out the shelves like you did the tops/ bottoms. Drill the shelf-pin holes. Cut the shelf pins to length and smooth the ends with sandpaper. After the cabinet is completed, remove the doors, sand all the parts up to 220-grit and apply the finish.

Jig for Routing a Hinge Mortise

STEP 1 Measure the distance from the bit to the edge of the router base. If you're using a guide collar, measure from the bit to the outside of the collar.

STEP 2 Measure the hinge's length and width. Add the measurement from step one to the width. Double the measurement from step one and add it to the length of the hinge. These are the two cutout sizes for the template's base.

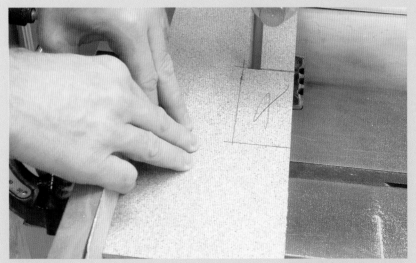

STEP 3 Use the measurements from step two and draw the cut out on the template's base. Make the first cut as shown.

STEP 4 Make a second cut to define the mortise's width.

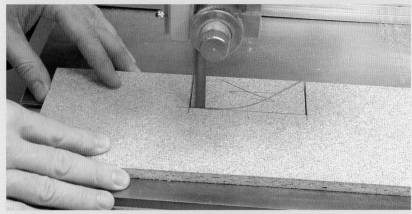

STEP 5 Make the first cut freehand, cutting up to the depth line.

STEP 6 Set the fence to the depth of the cutout and make the final cut.

STEP 7 Cut two cleats about 2" wide and as long as the template. These cleats are nailed or screwed to the template to hold it in place on the edge of the door, and they are great clamping blocks. Normally the edges of doors are square, but for this project the doors have beveled edges, so the cleats and the front edge of the template needed the same bevel. Use this jig as shown in steps 12 and 13.

Military Writing Desk

This ingenious box from the early 1800s folds open to reveal a leather surface that's ideal for writing letters.

supplies

Woodcraft Supply
(800) 225-1153
www.woodcraft.com
• Continuous Hinge,
2 - #152154, $7.99 ea.
• Quadrant Hinges,
#126965, $8.99 pr.
• Chest Straps,
8 - #127389, $9.50 pr.
• Adjustable ball catches,
#27H39, $3.75 each
• Lock, #130261 $12.50

Woodworker's Supply
(800) 645-9292
www.woodworker.com
• J.E. Moser's Light Shera-
ton Mahogany aniline dye,
#W13301, $10.99

Like a lot of Americans, I've recently been stricken with Lewis and Clark fever. I devoured Stephen Ambrose's book *Undaunted Courage*, watched the PBS special and am now wondering if my wife will let me hike the Lolo Trail. As you probably learned in history class, the primary record of Lewis and Clark's amazing trek to the mouth of the Columbia River is Meriwether Lewis's journal, which was a meticulous account of the flora and fauna they encountered on their trip.

How, I wondered, did explorers write their journals while blazing through the West? I haven't been able to find the answer to that question, but this desk is an educated guess. Traveling writing desks were common among British and American military officers of the day. They wrote their orders and journals on their portable desks, and when it was time to move the ranks, the desk was packed up and moved with the men.

This desk is an adaptation of a British military officer's desk from the early 19th century. And while you might not be writing orders to your left flank on this desk, it is quite handy for keeping up with all your correspondence. Personal or monarch-sized stationery stores in the area below the top; and pens, paper clips and envelopes fit nicely in the bottom section. Best of all, this project requires very little material. I made this one out of a 5'-long board of figured cherry. The originals were commonly built using mahogany.

Build the Box

The writing desk is essentially a box that has been cut on a diagonal line so that when it opens up, it forms a slanted writing surface. Now, a lot of box makers prefer gluing up a box and then

23

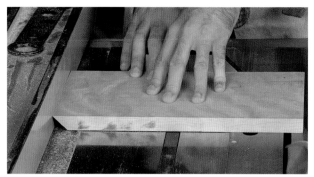

STEP 1 I cut my miters on the table saw, though you can use a chop saw if you please. Normally you're not supposed to use your rip fence and miter gauge simultaneously, but this is an exception. Set your saw's blade to a 45° angle and set your rip fence a little longer than the finished length of the board you're cutting. Now mark on your board the finished length of the piece. Make the cut with your saw, then move the rip fence in a little bit until the blade cuts right to the mark. Now turn the piece of wood around and cut the opposite side. Repeat this process for the smaller sides.

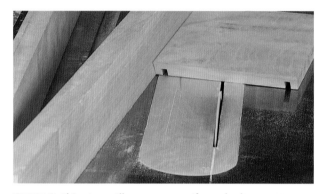

STEP 2 This step will mess you up if you don't pay attention. First dry assemble your four sides and mark approximately where the angles will go. Then take the pieces to the table saw. Remember: One side will have to be cut with the miters down against the saw's table and the other side will have to be cut with the miters facing up.

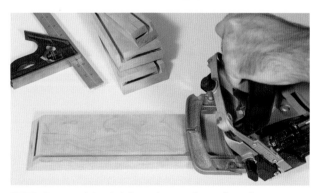

STEP 3 Most biscuit joiners have a fence that allows you to cut this joint as shown in the photo. If not, try this trick. Clamp one mitered piece to the piece it will be joined to so that the two miters form a perfect V between them. Then put your biscuit joiner in the V and cut the slot on one side. Turn the tool to the other miter and make the same cut.

cutting the thing apart on the table saw to separate the lid from the base. That won't work here. Because the cut is on the diagonal, you either have to build the two parts separately (as I did) or glue up the box and cut the two pieces apart on a band saw that has a generous resawing capacity.

The box itself is simple. The four sides are mitered and then glued together using biscuit joints and polyurethane glue. The top and bottom are merely raised panels captured in a groove in the sides.

Begin by cutting your pieces to the sizes shown in the Schedule of Materials. Next cut the miters on the ends of the four pieces as shown in step 1.

Now cut the ⅜"-deep by ¼"-wide groove along the top and bottom edges of all four sides with a dado stack in your table saw. The groove should begin ⁵⁄₁₆" from each edge. This will recess your ½"-thick panels ¹⁄₁₆" in from the edges and will keep the panels from rubbing against tabletops. Now cut the panels to finished size and raise them using either a table saw or router in a router table. You want the edges to finish out at about ³⁄₁₆" thick.

Cut the Angles

The trick to cutting the two short sides at an angle is to make sure that the cut begins in the dead center of the back of the board. That's because you want your desk to lay flat when you open it. Set your table saw's tapering jig to 9° and try your setup with some scrap first. When satisfied, cut the short sides.

Now set your table saw's blade to 9° and rip the long sides. This will allow the long sides to mate with the angled short sides. You absolutely must test your setup with scrap pieces before you make these cuts.

Biscuits All Around

Except for two of the corners, a no. 10 biscuit will fit on all of the miters. I used a mini-biscuit cutter for the two narrow sides. You could use dowels instead. Cut all the slots for the biscuits, then dry assemble the two boxes. When satisfied with the fit, sand everything, especially the two panels and the parts that face inside the box. I started with 120-grit sandpaper and finished with 220.

Some tips for gluing up the top and bottom: First, polyurethane glue is an excellent choice for this short-grain joint. Just make sure you dip each biscuit in water before putting it in its slot and be sure to add

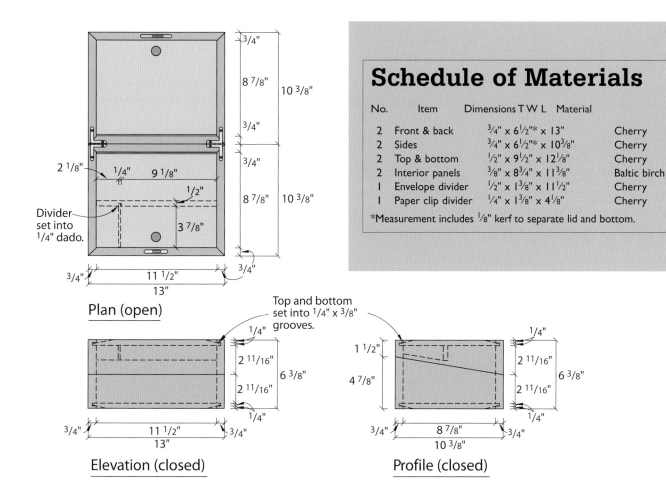

Plan (open)

3/4"
8 7/8"
10 3/8"
3/4"
3/4"
2 1/8"
1/4"
9 1/8"
1/2"
8 7/8"
10 3/8"
Divider set into 1/4" dado.
3 7/8"
3/4"
11 1/2"
3/4"
13"

Schedule of Materials

No.	Item	Dimensions T W L	Material
2	Front & back	3/4" x 6 1/2"* x 13"	Cherry
2	Sides	3/4" x 6 1/2"* x 10 3/8"	Cherry
2	Top & bottom	1/2" x 9 1/2" x 12 1/8"	Cherry
2	Interior panels	3/8" x 8 3/4" x 11 3/8"	Baltic birch
1	Envelope divider	1/2" x 1 3/8" x 11 1/2"	Cherry
1	Paper clip divider	1/4" x 1 3/8" x 4 1/8"	Cherry

*Measurement includes 1/8" kerf to separate lid and bottom.

Elevation (closed)

Top and bottom set into 1/4" x 3/8" grooves.
1/4"
2 11/16"
6 3/8"
2 11/16"
1/4"
3/4"
11 1/2"
3/4"
13"

Profile (closed)

1 1/2"
4 7/8"
1/4"
2 11/16"
6 3/8"
2 11/16"
1/4"
3/4"
8 7/8"
3/4"
10 3/8"

a little water to each joint to speed up the curing. Polyurethane glue has a long open time, so you have plenty of time to get your clamps just right. When all of your miters are tight, measure each box corner to corner to make sure everything is square. Let the glue cure overnight.

Now glue some pieces of smooth leather or felt to the two interior panels. Yellow glue works fine. I attached the leather using the same method many woodworkers use to glue up veneer, sandwiching the leather between two panels. Attach small piano hinges to one of the long edges of each panel and attach them to the inside of the box. Add small stops inside the box to support each panel. I cut a 7/8" hole in each panel so I can easily open the two compartments in the box. To hold the panels in place when you close the box, I highly recommend buying a couple adjustable ball catches (available in most woodworking catalogs for about $2.50 each). Really, though, you also could use almost any other cabinet catch.

Now it's time to join the two boxes using quadrant hinges. Most quadrant hinges have a metal bar that runs between the two leaves to prevent people from opening a box's lid too far. Remove or cut these small

bars off; you want your hinges to open all the way. Now attach the chest straps to the outside corners of the box so that when you attach your hinges you've taken into account the space the straps will add. Trust me, it's important. Mortise the quadrant hinges into the top and bottom. Close the box and sand your joints flush.

Shape and then glue the envelope divider and paper clip divider in place in the shallow side. Mortise a chest lock into the top and bottom. Remove all the hardware and begin finishing. I used a water-based aniline dye and followed that with two coats of clear finish. Then I wiped on a thin coat of warm brown glaze to remove some of the orange color of the red finish. Finally, I added another two coats of clear finish, sanding between coats. This finish, which takes a little patience, gives the cherry a warmth that is worth more than the extra effort.

Now I just have to talk my wife into letting me hike the Lolo Trail. I could bring the desk along and write to her about my journey, my bug bites, my aching feet — all from the same remote and lonely campsites used by Lewis and Clark. Or maybe I'll just stick to trailblazing my backyard.

Entertainment Center

by Glen Huey

Entertainment centers were not a part of 18th-century homes. The need for a cupboard to house a television and stereo equipment did not exist. But utility cupboards occupied nearly every home, and excellent examples are available today.

This piece is one of those examples. The drawers set below the doors are a natural place to store DVDs or CDs. The doors open completely so there is open access to the electronic equipment, making it a perfect location for the television and you can add as many adjustable shelves as you need.

The construction also is easy to customize. Adding depth to the cabinet is simple and does not change the overall look. The frame-and-panel design lends itself to maintaining an antique look while accounting for panel movement from seasonal changes. This is one piece that you will enjoy building and living with while it holds today's most prominent household appliance.

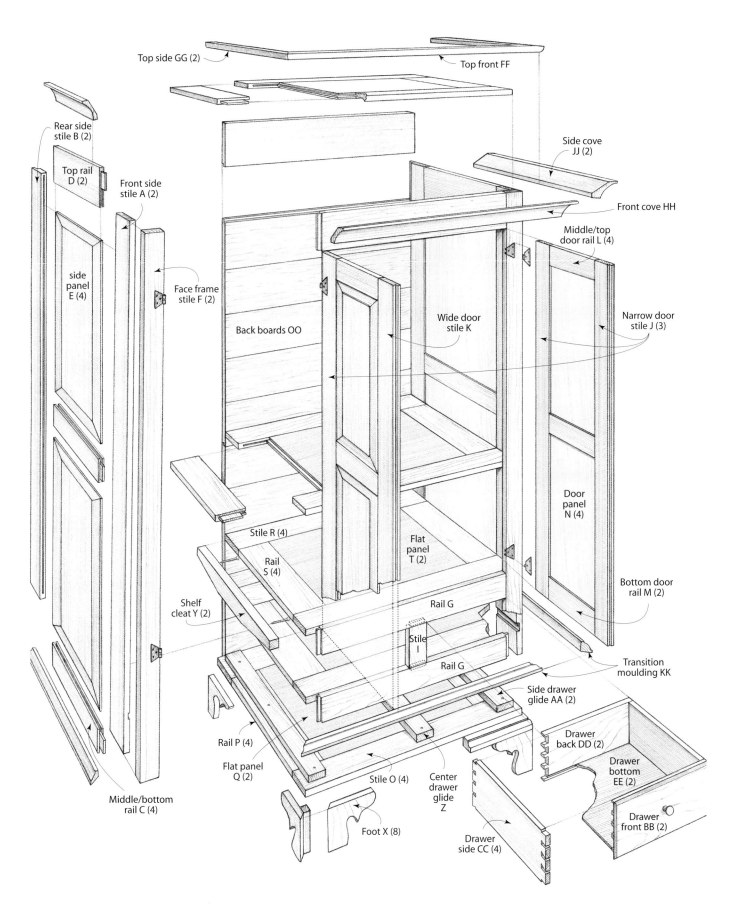

Top side GG (2)

Top front FF

Rear side
stile B (2)

Side cove
JJ (2)

Top rail
D (2)

Front side
stile A (2)

Front cove HH

Middle/top
door rail L (4)

side
panel
E (4)

Face frame
stile F (2)

Back boards OO

Wide door
stile K

Narrow door
stile J (3)

Door
panel
N (4)

Stile R (4)

Flat
panel
T (2)

Rail
S (4)

Shelf
cleat Y (2)

Rail G

Bottom door
rail M (2)

Stile
I

Rail G

Transition
moulding KK

Side drawer
glide AA (2)

Rail P (4)

Drawer
back DD (2)

Flat panel
Q (2)

Stile O (4)

Center
drawer
glide
Z

Drawer
bottom
EE (2)

Middle/bottom
rail C (4)

Foot X (8)

Drawer
side CC (4)

Drawer
front BB (2)

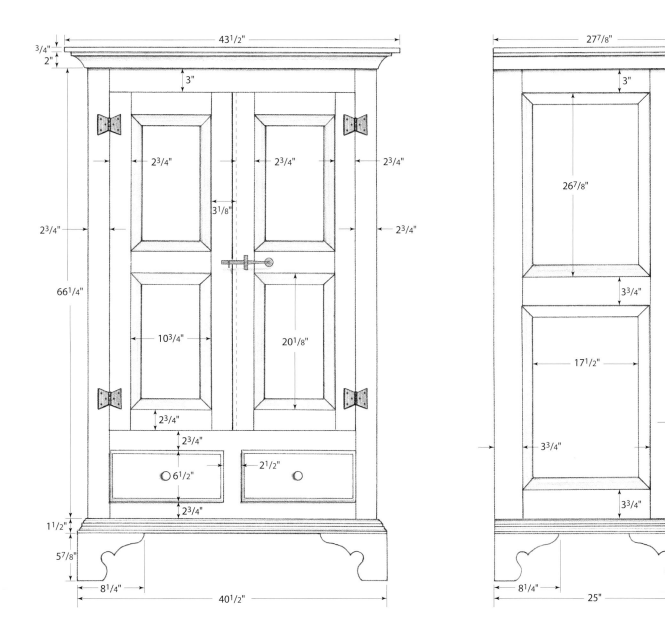

cutting list

	QUANTITY	PART	STOCK	THICKNESS		WIDTH		LENGTH		COMMENTS
A	2	front side stiles	poplar	¾	(19)	3	(76)	66¼	(1683)	
B	2	rear side stiles	poplar	¾	(19)	3¾	(95)	66¼	(1683)	
C	4	middle and bottom rails	poplar	¾	(19)	3¾	(95)	20	(508)	1¼" (32mm) tenon both ends
D	2	top rails	poplar	¾	(19)	5	(127)	20	(508)	1¼" (32mm) tenon both ends
E	4	raised cabinet panels	poplar	⅝	(16)	18⅛	(460)	27½	(699)	
F	2	face-frame stiles	poplar	¾	(19)	2¾	(70)	66¼	(1683)	
G	2	face-frame rails	poplar	¾	(19)	2¾	(70)	35	(889)	1¼" (32mm) tenon both ends
H	1	face-top rail	poplar	¾	(19)	5	(127)	35	(889)	1¼" (32mm) tenon both ends
I	1	drawer divider	poplar	¾	(19)	2½	(64)	9	(229)	1¼" (32mm) tenon both ends
J	3	narrow door stiles	poplar	¾	(19)	2¾	(70)	49¼	(1251)	
K	1	wide door stile	poplar	¾	(19)	3⅛	(79)	49¼	(1251)	
L	4	middle & top door rails	poplar	¾	(19)	2¾	(70)	13¼	(337)	1¼" (32mm) tenon both ends
M	2	bottom door rails	poplar	¾	(19)	3½	(89)	13¼	(337)	1¼" (32mm) tenon both ends
N	2	raised door panels	poplar	⅝	(16)	11⅜	(289)	20¾	(527)	

Case top and bottom panels

O	4	stiles	poplar	¾	(19)	3	(76)	37	(940)	
P	4	rails	poplar	¾	(19)	5	(127)	20	(508)	1¼" (32mm) tenon both ends
Q	2	flat panels	poplar	¾	(19)	18⅛	(460)	27⅝	(702)	

Shelves

R	4	stiles	poplar	¾	(19)	3	(76)	36⅜	(924)	
S	4	rails	poplar	¾	(19)	5	(127)	19	(483)	1¼" (32mm) tenon both ends
T	2	flat panels	poplar	¾	(19)	17⅛	(435)	27	(686)	
U	1	base-frame front	poplar	¾	(19)	3	(76)	40¼	(1022)	miter cut both ends
V	2	base-frame sides	poplar	¾	(19)	3	(76)	26⅛	(664)	miter cut one end
W	1	base-frame back	poplar	¾	(19)	3	(76)	36¾	(933)	1¼" (32mm) tenon both ends
X	8	feet	poplar	¾	(19)	5⅞	(149)	8¼	(210)	6 cut to pattern
Y	2	shelf cleats	poplar	¾	(19)	2	(51)	23	(584)	
Z	1	center drawer glide	poplar	¾	(19)	2½	(64)	23	(584)	
AA	2	outside drawer glides	poplar	¾	(19)	1	(25)	23	(584)	
BB	2	drawer fronts	poplar	¾	(19)	6¾	(171)	15⅝	(397)	
CC	4	drawer sides	poplar	½	(13)	6⅜	(162)	20	(508)	
DD	2	drawer backs	poplar	½	(13)	5⅝	(143)	14⅞	(378)	
EE	2	drawer bottoms	poplar	⅝	(16)	20	(508)	15	(381)	cut to fit

Mouldings

FF	1	top front	poplar	¾	(19)	3¾	(95)	43½	(1105)	miter cut both ends
GG	2	top sides	poplar	¾	(19)	3¾	(95)	27⅞	(708)	miter cut one end
HH	1	front cove	poplar	¾	(19)	3	(76)	44	(1118)	miter cut both ends
JJ	2	side coves	poplar	¾	(19)	3	(76)	29	(737)	miter cut one end
KK	2	transition	poplar	¾	(19)	1½	(38)	52	(1320)	makes 2 pieces
LL	1	interior door catch	poplar	⅝	(16)	¾	(19)	2½	(64)	
MM	1	top door stop	poplar	⅝	(16)	2¾	(70)	3½	(89)	
NN	1	bottom door stop	poplar	¾	(19)	¾	(19)	2¾	(70)	
OO		back boards	poplar	⅝	(16)	65	(1651)	37½	(953)	random width boards

hardware & supplies

- 4—2½" (65mm) × 3"(75mm) door hinges, black iron
- 1—door catch, black iron
- 2—1⅛" (30mm) door knobs, black iron
- nails, clout or shingle

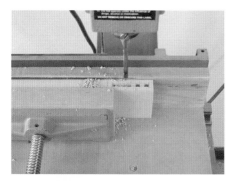

STEP 1 The case sides are made with a series of mortise and tenons that are fitted with raised panels. Lay out the mortise locations on the stiles of the case sides cut to size from the cutting list. Create the ¼" × 3" × 1¼" (6mm × 76mm × 32mm) slots for the middle and bottom rail tenons as well as the ¼" × 4¼" × 1¼" (6mm × 108mm × 32mm) slots for the top rail tenons. Use the step method of cutting the mortises. Cut every other ¼" (6mm)× ¼" (6mm) hole from end to end on your mortise, then return to remove the balance of the material on a second pass. This keeps equal pressure on all sides of the mortising chisel and bit sets and reduces undo ware.

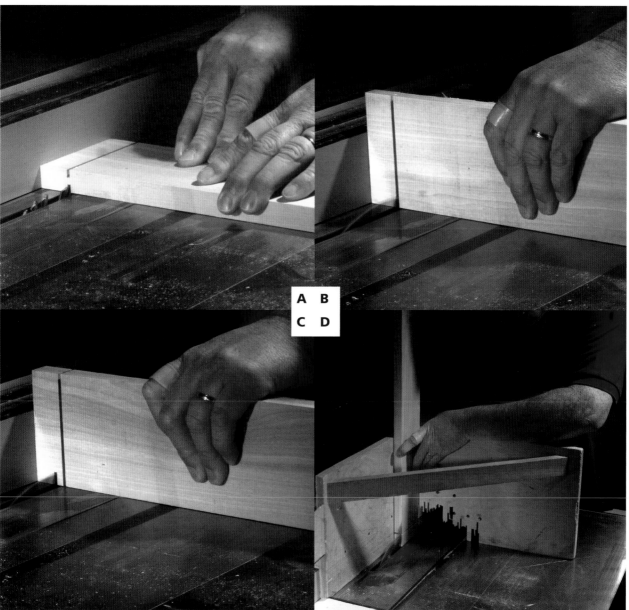

A   B
C   D

STEP 2 Here's how to make the tenons using the table saw: Set the blade to ¼" (6mm) in height and the fence at 1¼" (32mm) (this includes the width of the blade). Make a cut on each flat side of all rails for the two sides (Photo a). Then raise the blade height to ⅜" (10mm) and don't change the fence setting. Cut one edge on the top and bottom rails and both edges of the middle rails (Photo b). Next, move the fence ⅜" towards the blade and cut the uncut edges (Photo c). (This creates the haunch area that fills the groove for the panels.) Use a tenoning fixture to cut the tenons to fit into the mortises (Photo d). Cut equal amounts from each face to center the tenon on the rails.

STEP 3 Cut the tenons to width using the band saw. Note the haunch at the top of the tenon.

STEP 4 Use the table saw to cut the groove for the raised panels. Set the height to ³⁄₈". (This matches the haunched portion of the tenon.) Set the fence at a ¼". Make a pass along each piece of the frame, reverse the pieces, make a second pass, cutting the groove at ¼" wide. This will center the groove in the rails and stiles. Fine-tune this cut, if necessary, so the tenons fit into the grooves. The inset shows the completed mortise-and-tenon joint. The haunch will fit into the groove, filling in any opening.

STEP 5 Mill the cabinet panels to thickness. Dry fit a side frame. Measure the inside width and height of the panel openings and add ⁵⁄₈" to each dimension. Tilt the table saw blade to 12°, set the fence at ³⁄₁₆" from the blade at its lowest point (flush with the tabletop) and raise the blade just high enough to make the cut. I recommend using an extended fence for this procedure. It allows you to clamp the panel to the fence to hold it steady. Cut all four edges of the panel.

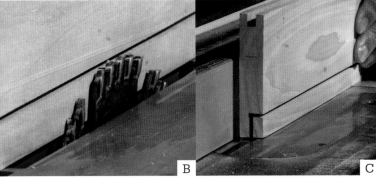

B

C

STEP 6 To cut the rabbet on the inside rear edge of the rear side stiles, set the saw blade height to $7/16$" and the fence to $3/4$" (including the blade's width). Make the cut. Now set the blade height to $3/4$" and the fence so the rabbet is $7/16$". (The fence setting at this stage will depend on the thickness of the material.)

A

A

STEP 7 Sand the panels with 180-grit sandpaper, add glue into the mortises and on each tenon and assemble the case sides. Then fit the joints together for one half of the frames. Slide the panels into the groove and slip the balance of the frame together. Add clamps to complete the first side. Repeat the steps for the second side and allow the glue to dry.

B

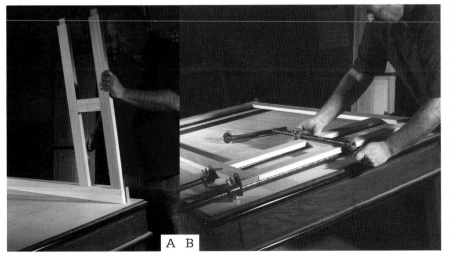

A B

STEP 8 Mill the parts for the face frame to size according to the cutting list and cut the mortises in the top, middle and bottom rails. You also need to cut a mortise in the bottom and middle rails for the drawer divider. Next, cut the tenons on the rails and the drawer divider as you did in step 2. This time the blade height is set at $1/4$". Make cuts on all four sides of each rail. Then use the tenoning fixture to cut the tenons to thickness and width. With the joints cut and fit, assemble the face frame as shown.

STEP 9 The top and bottom panels as well as the shelves are more lessons in mortise-and-tenon joinery. You will create the mortises, tenons and grooves just as you did for the cabinet sides. However, instead of a raised panel, these parts have flat panels. They are made by cutting a rabbet (as shown in step 8) on both sides of the flat panel. The resulting tongue is ¼" thick and ¼" long. Assemble the parts using glue only at the frame's joints.

STEP 10 Cut a groove for the top and bottom panels. Use a straightedge and a ¾" pattern bit to cut the grooves. The groove for the top panel is 1" down from the top edge of the case. The bottom panel is flush with the top edge of the bottom face-frame rail. Install the panels in the grooves and attach with No. 8 × 1¼" screws.

STEP 11 Lay the cabinet on its back and position the face frame on the cabinet. Using glue and clamps, attach the face frame to the cabinet.

STEP 12 When the glue has dried, use a router with a bottom-mount bearing to trim the face frame flush to the side of the cabinet.

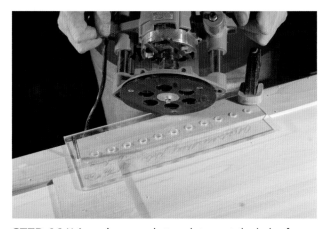

STEP 13 The shelf cleats are attached to the cabinet's side stiles with No. 8 × 1¼" screws. Locate the cleats so the shelf rests ¼" above the middle rail of the face frame. The shelf will act as a stop for the doors.

STEP 14 Using a homemade template, rout the holes for the shelf pins. Be sure to locate the template at the same height for each set of holes. This step will assures the shelves are both level and secure.

STEP 15 Install the drawer glides to the cabinet bottom. Attach the two side glides using brads and glue. The center glide is attached with screws to the front and rear stiles of the bottom panel.

STEP 16 Slide one of the shelves onto the shelf cleats and hold it tight to the case front as you attach it to the cleat using screws.

STEP 17 Sand the cabinet. This is to be a painted piece so there is no need to go beyond 150-grit sandpaper.

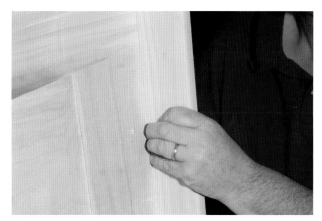

STEP 18 To make the top mouldings, use a ½" roundover bit to rout a bullnose on one edge of the moulding. The moulding overhangs the cabinet ¾" and is attached to the top of the cabinet using screws. Glue and biscuits keep the mitered corners tight.

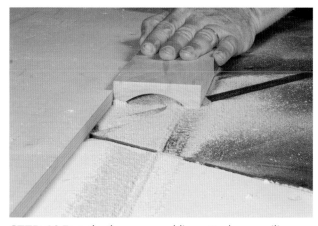

STEP 19 To make the cove moulding, attach an auxiliary fence to the table saw top at an angle to the blade. Make ¹⁄₁₆" cuts on each pass. Raise the blade until you reach the desired depth of cut.

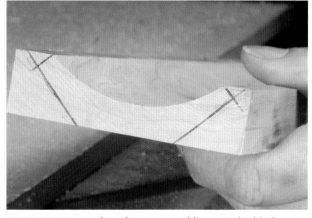

STEP 20 To complete the cove moulding, set the blade to 45° and make the two longer cuts with the stock face up and flat on the tabletop. To make the smaller cuts, set the blade to 90°. Place the long cut edge against the fence to complete the moulding.

STEP 21 Cut the corners of the cove moulding at 45° and fit them to the case. Attach the moulding using brads at both the top and bottom edges of the cove.

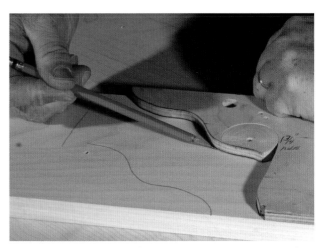

STEP 22 Cut the blanks for the feet. Make the pattern of ¼"-thick plywood. Trace the profile on six of the foot blanks. Mark the center point of the drilled area.

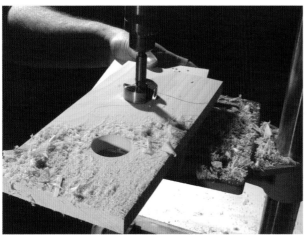

STEP 23 Use a 1¾" Forstner bit to cut holes in the feet. These holes will form the spur of the foot.

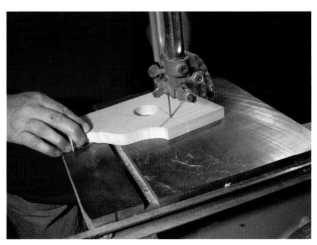

STEP 24 Cut the profiles using a band saw, then sand the edges smooth.

STEP 25 Cut the miters on the two right-handed feet.

STEP 26 Reverse the miter gauge and cut the two left-handed feet as shown. For safety reasons, do not try to cut the left feet using the set up in step 25.

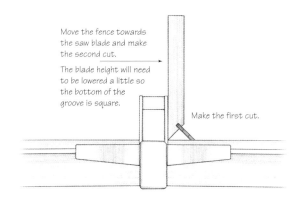
Move the fence towards the saw blade and make the second cut.

The blade height will need to be lowered a little so the bottom of the groove is square.

Make the first cut.

STEP 27 Cut a slot for splines into each of the mitered feet. Keep the blade at the 45° angle. Change the height of the blade and reposition the fence to cut the slot. Make two passes on each foot to create the ¼" slot. As you adjust the fence for the second cut, it's necessary to adjust the height of the blade. If the fence is moved toward the blade, the height will decrease. The opposite is true if you move away from the blade. See the illustration for details.

STEP 28 Add glue to the slots and the face of the miter cuts. Insert the plywood spline and assemble the foot. I like to wrap the assembly with duct tape to hold it until the glue dries.

STEP 29 In the back edge of the two profiled feet, cut a rabbet that will accept the unprofiled foot. Then make a 45° cut on the unprofiled foot.

STEP 30 Glue and screw the back foot assemblies together.

STEP 31 Cut the parts for the base frame. Miter the front corners and make a mortise-and-tenon joint for the intersection of the back and sides. Use a biscuit joiner to cut a slot for No.20 biscuits in the mitered cuts.

STEP 32 Assemble the mortise-and-tenon joints first, then add glue for the biscuits. Make sure the clamps from front to back are centered on the mortise-and-tenon joint. Apply even pressure to all four clamps. Check the assembly for squareness.

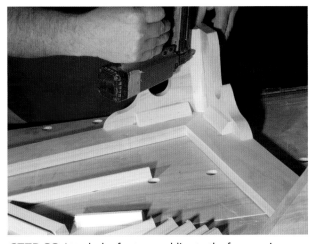

STEP 33 Attach the foot assemblies to the frame using glue, and hold the foot in place with a clamp. Then, using glue and brads, install the glue blocks. The glue blocks add tremendous strength to the foot assemblies.

STEP 34 To complete the base assembly, rout a profile on the edges of the sides and front of the frame's edges. Then, sand the entire base. Next, position the cabinet on the frame and draw the outline of the outside of the cabinet on it. To mark where the screws can be installed when the base is attached to the cabinet, predrill ⅜" holes inside the line.

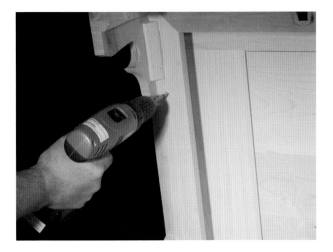

STEP 35 Lay the cabinet on its back and position the base on the cabinet. Countersink the holes drilled in step 34. Then, using No.8 × 1¼" screws, attach the base to the cabinet.

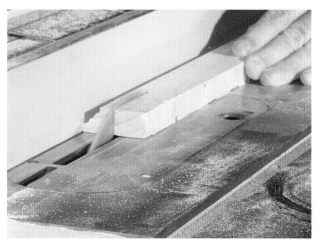

STEP 36 Rout the profile of the transition moulding on double-wide stock, then rip the stock to the final width of the moulding.

STEP 37 The transition moulding covers the joint of the base frame and the cabinet. It has a 45° mitered connection at the front corners. The back is cut flush with the rear edge of the cabinet's back. Attach the moulding using glue and brads.

STEP 38 The doors are assembled using mortise-and-tenon joinery and raised panels like the cabinet sides. Decide whether the right or left door will be operable and which will be latched. The latched door will need the wider door stile (in the center of the door). I made the right-hand door operable. I positioned the wider stile on the right-hand side of the left door.

STEP 39 This photo shows the lap joint at the center stiles of the doors. The left door is latched, so its center stile needs a rabbet in order for the operable door to overlap it when the doors are closed. (The overlap is ⅜".) The latched door will be rabbeted on the face side and the other door on the back side.

STEP 40 Cut the dovetail joinery in the drawer backs and sides. The lipped drawer fronts are joined to the sides with half-blind dovetails. After cutting the ⅜" × ½" rabbet on the top and side edges of the drawer fronts, scribe a line that is equal to the thickness of the sides on the inside of the drawer fronts.

Cutting The Dove-tail Sockets

define the dovetails (a)

Layout the dovetails (I use a 12° angle) on the ends of the fronts and extend the lines about 1½" towards the center of the fronts. These are the lines you cut to define the edges of the dovetail sockets. Be careful not to nick the drawer lip. Cut down the lines as far as possible. This will mean less to clear with the chisels.

removing material (b)

Visable overcut from the saw is acceptable and seen in any number of museum collections of furniture. Place the chisel in front of the scribed line and set the cut. As you hit the chisel, it will move toward the line. Set the cut across each of the sockets. Then remove the waste material with a chisel. The corners of the pins (the remaining material after the socket is created) are fragile and easily knocked off. To remove the waste, take small bites starting at the corners of the socket. Keep the chisel at a 45° angle to remove each corner as shown, then remove the middle area of the socket.

depth of sockets (c)

Repeat these steps of removing the waste until the bottom of the socket is set. It should be flush with the lip of the drawer.

width of sockets (d)

Use a ½" chisel to pare down the sides of the sockets to the layout lines. This will become the pattern for the dovetails that fit these sockets, i.e., the look of the completed dovetail joint for the drawer. Make them look great!

back of sockets (e)

Use a ¼" chisel to trim the back corners of the sockets. Make sure that the back wall of the socket angles away from the edge at a 2° slope. This will help to close the joint when it is assembled.

finished sockets

When the dovetail sockets are completed, the drawer front is set onto the scribed drawer sides and the socket layout is transferred to the sides. Cut the tails.

finished dovetail sockets

STEP 42 Complete the drawers by cutting the groove in the bottoms and installing them using a square nail.

STEP 43 The beginning of the finishing process is to apply a coat of water-based aniline dye, lightly sand with 400-grit paper to smooth the raised grain and apply two coats of shellac. There are two reasons for doing this. One, it seals the wood to allow better manipulation of the paint and, two, it provides a finish for the interior of the piece. I use an acrylic latex paint. Before applying the paint, give it texture by adding fine sawdust.

STEP 44 Work a small area at a time. Here, I'm working on one of the doors. Apply the paint to the surface and allow it to dry a bit. The direction of the paint strokes will show on the finished project so I like to paint in the direction of the wood grain.

STEP 45 Once the paint has dried a little, use a clean wet rag to simulate worn areas (rub the surface to let the stain show in some places). The sawdust helps the rag grab the paint. Be careful because a little aging goes a long way.

STEP 46 If you find that you have overdone the "aging" a bit, one of the great things about this process is that you can add more paint.

STEP 47 This photo shows how the sawdust creeps into corners and builds up to simulate aging. I chose hand-hammered black iron for hardware. The butterfly hinges are a great period look, as is the latch. Once the doors are hung, you need to add the door stops and the catch. The catch is a piece of wood that is screwed to inside of the door and swivels to catch the face frame when the door is closed.

STEP 48 The backboards have shiplap joinery. There is no finish on these pieces, so as they age, they get their own patina. The boards run horizontally and are nailed to the case sides. Gapping between them depends on the time of year the cabinet is built because they will expand and contract with seasonal changes. Each board has one nail per case side, but the top and bottom boards have two nails per side.

STEP 49 A protective coat or two of paste wax can add a sheen to the painted finish.

Franklin Chair

by John McGuane

Legend has it that the design for this ingenious piece of furniture, also known as a ladder chair or library chair, was invented by Benjamin Franklin. This attractive, useful chair easily converts into a ladder, enabling you to reach the top shelves of bookcases and cabinets without having to pull your stepladder out of storage.

This project is made of yellow pine purchased at a local home-improvement center. I used yellow pine because of its strength and stability. Although I finished my Franklin chair with shellac, it can be painted to fit any room or decor.

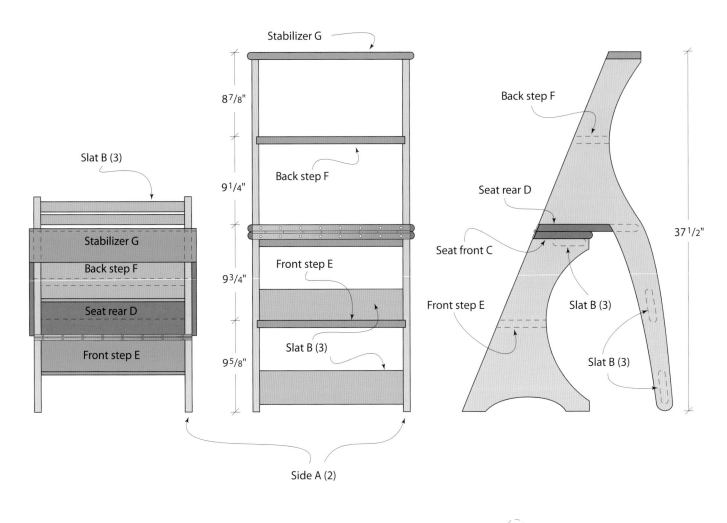

Slat B (3)

Stabilizer G
Back step F
Seat rear D
Front step E

Stabilizer G

8 7/8"

Back step F

9 1/4"

Front step E

9 3/4"

Slat B (3)

9 5/8"

Side A (2)

Back step F

Seat rear D

Seat front C

Front step E

Slat B (3)

Slat B (3)

37 1/2"

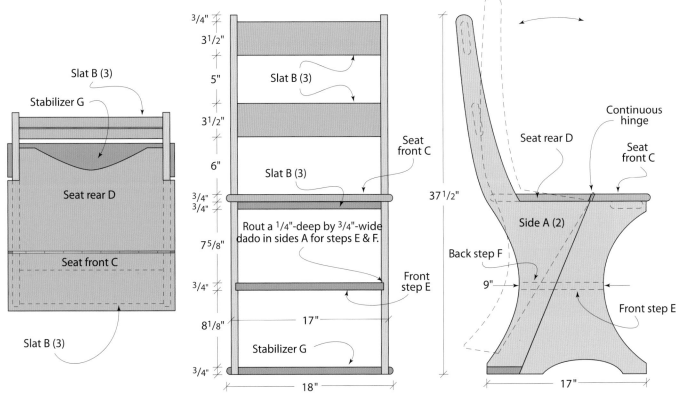

Slat B (3)

Stabilizer G

Seat rear D

Seat front C

Slat B (3)

3/4"

3 1/2"

Slat B (3)

5"

3 1/2"

Slat B (3)

6"

3/4"
3/4"

Rout a 1/4"-deep by 3/4"-wide
dado in sides A for steps E & F.

7 5/8"

3/4"

17"

8 1/8"

Stabilizer G

3/4"

18"

Seat
front C

Front
step E

Continuous
hinge

Seat rear D

Seat
front C

37 1/2"

Side A (2)

Back step F

9"

Front step E

17"

cutting list

INCHES (MILLIMETERS)

REFERENCE	QUANTITY	PART	STOCK	THICKNESS	(mm)	WIDTH	(mm)	LENGTH	(mm)	COMMENTS
A	2	sides	yellow pine	$3/4$	(19)	$20^{1}/4$	(514)	$37^{1}/2$	(953)	
B	3	rails	yellow pine	$3/4$	(19)	$3^{1}/2$	(89)	$15^{1}/2$	(394)	
C	1	seat front	yellow pine	$3/4$	(19)	18	(457)	$6^{5}/16$	(160)	23° bevel on hinge edge
D	1	seat rear	yellow pine	$3/4$	(19)	18	(457)	$10^{7}/8$	(276)	23° bevel on hinge edge
E	1	front step	yellow pine	$3/4$	(19)	$5^{1}/8$	(130)	16	(406)	23° bevel on one long edge
F	1	back step	yellow pine	$3/4$	(19)	$4^{1}/4$	(108)	16	(406)	23° bevel on one long edge
G	1	top stabilizer	yellow pine	$3/4$	(19)	$3^{3}/4$	(95)	$17^{1}/2$	(445)	

HARDWARE & SUPPLIES

1	$17^{3}/4$" (451mm) brass-plated continuous hinge
28	$3/8$"-diameter x $1/4$"-long (10mm x 6mm) maple plugs
28	No. 10 x 2" (51mm) steel screws
10-20	No. 20 biscuits
	wood glue

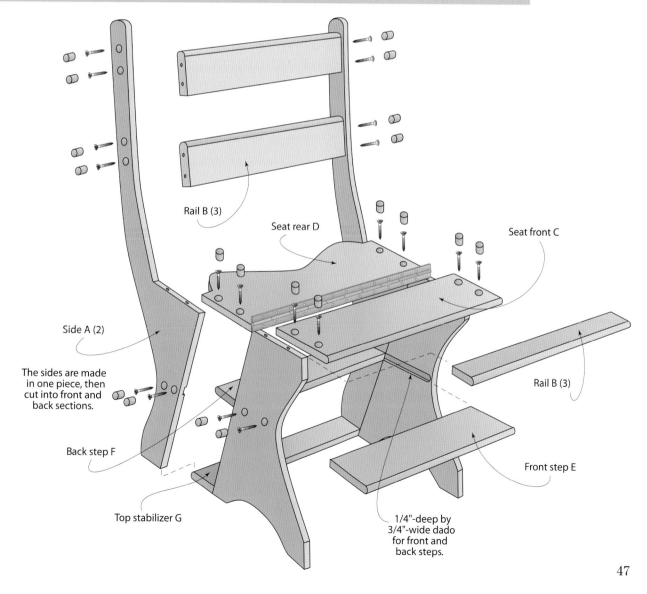

Rail B (3)

Seat rear D

Seat front C

Side A (2)

The sides are made in one piece, then cut into front and back sections.

Back step F

Rail B (3)

Front step E

Top stabilizer G

1/4"-deep by 3/4"-wide dado for front and back steps.

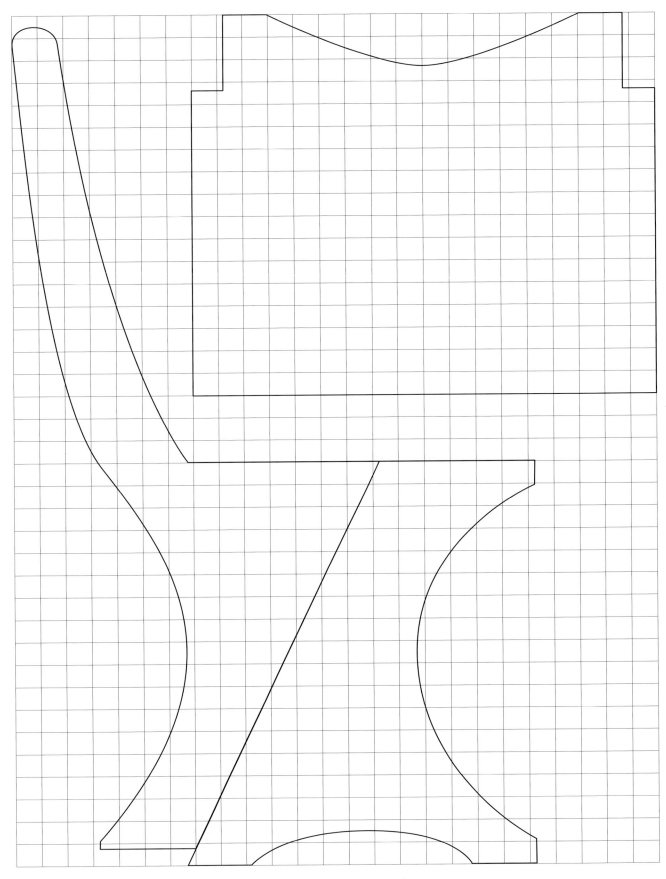

Each square represents 1".

STEP 1 The yellow pine for this project was purchased from a local home-improvement center. Yellow pine is strong and stable when properly seasoned. It's an excellent material for projects that require strength and rigidity.

This folding ladder was the model for the Franklin chair.

STEP 2 Use your compound miter saw to cut the boards to the proper lengths. Then cut the slots for the biscuits. Be sure the location of the biscuits won't be on the cutting line of the side pattern.

Tip

Chairs and ladders need to support a wide range of loads. Think carefully when you build anything that would cause an injury if a failure in design or workmanship should occur. Pay special attention to your load-supporting joints. I reinforced all the joints of this project with 2" steel screws. The screw heads are countersunk and plugged. The screws make assembly much easier, as clamping is not required.

STEP 3 Use battens to help keep the glued-up sides flat.

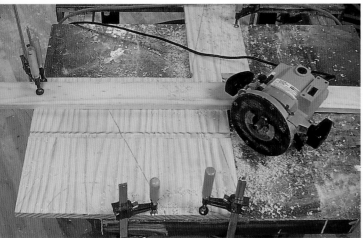

STEP 4 Glue the final wing piece on the long back edges of the sides. Then, using a straightedge and a router, cut a 1/4"-deep by 3/4"-wide dado in the sides for the front and back steps. Be sure to make right and left sides.

STEP 5 Draw the pattern on the side blanks (see pattern illustration). Then, using a jigsaw, separate the front and back parts of the sides.

STEP 6 This side pattern is one idea of how the chair could look. Feel free to change this pattern to suit your tastes.

STEP 7 The jigsaw is a good tool for cutting the patterns on the sides. You could also use a band saw or coping saw.

STEP 8 Finish cutting the back part of the sides.

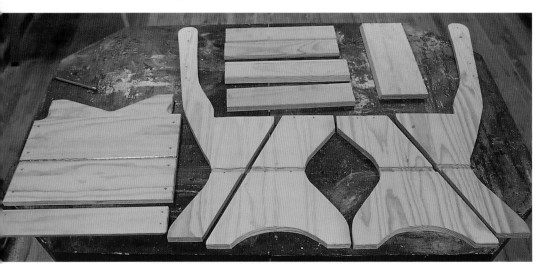

STEP 9 Use your own sense of design when laying out the curves on your chair. Just be careful not to compromise strength by removing too much material. You can use a bucket or other round object to help lay out the curves.

STEP 10 Cut the steps and slats to size and check the fit of all the parts. Sand them before final assembly.

STEP 11 Assemble the chair using glue and screws.

STEP 12 After cutting the seat to shape, separate the front and back parts. Then attach the continuous hinge to the parts. The bevels on the hinged edges of the seat should match the angle of the front and back parts of the chair sides. Finally, attach the seat to the chair, using glue and screws. Plug all the screws holes on the chair and sand them flush.

STEP 13 Finish the chair how you like. I used three coats of shellac.

Drop-Front Secretary

by Jim Stack

The drop-front is a traditional piece of furniture found in most farm houses and homes built in the early 20th century and is ideally located in a living room, bedroom, den or office. However, I remember seeing a tired-looking drop-front desk in an equally tired-looking barn. I felt bad for them both.

Variations in design can include locks on the doors, drawers instead of a door in the lower section below the drop desktop and a plywood back with veneer taped edges.

cutting list

INCHES (MILLIMETERS)

REFERENCE	QUANTITY	PART	STOCK	THICKNESS		WIDTH		LENGTH		COMMENTS
A	1	left side	cherry	¾	(19)	12	(305)	52¾	(1320)	⅜" (10mm) tenon both ends (tbe)
B	1	center partition	cherry	¾	(19)	11¼	(246)	52¾	(1320)	⅜" (10mm) tbe, mortise right side
C	1	right side	cherry	¾	(19)	12	(305)	35¾	(908)	⅜" (10mm) tbe, tapered to top
D	1	bottom	cherry	¾	(19)	13½	(343)	40¼	(1022)	three dadoes
E	1	left top	cherry	¾	(19)	12¾	(337)	20¾	(527)	two dadoes
F	1	right top	cherry	¾	(19)	9	(229)	20	(508)	one dado, ⅜" (10mm) tenon one end
G	1	desk shelf	cherry	¾	(19)	10½	(267)	19¼	(489)	⅜" (10mm) tbe
H	1	front rail	cherry	¾	(19)	3½	(89)	20⅜	(518)	both ends notched. miter right end
I	1	attached moulding*	cherry	⅜	(10)	¾	(19)	13*	(330)	miter one end, *cut length to fit
J	2	base front and back	cherry	¾	(19)	4	(102)	39½	(997)	mitered both ends
K	2	base ends	cherry	¾	(19)	4	(102)	12	(305)	mitered both ends
L	4	feet	cherry	3	(76)	3	(76)	8¾	(222)	
M	2	corner blocks	cherry	¾	(19)	3	(76)	3	(76)	
N	2	cleats	cherry	¾	(19)	¾	(19)	32	(813)	
P	2	cleats	cherry	¾	(19)	¾	(19)	7	(178)	
Q	4	shelves*	cherry	¾	(19)	11	(279)	18⁷⁄₁₆	(468)	*or ¼ (6mm) tempered glass shelves
Back										
R	2	stiles	cherry	¾	(19)	3	(76)	58	(1473)	cut to length after back is assembled
S	1	center stile	cherry	¾	(19)	3	(76)	48	(1219)	¾" (19mm) tbe
T	1	crest rail	cherry	¾	(19)	12	(76)	34½	(876)	¾" (19mm) tbe
U	1	bottom rail	cherry	¾	(19)	3	(76)	34½	(876)	¾" (19mm) tbe
V	2	panels	cherry	½	(13)	15⅝	(397)	47	(1194)	
Cubby Assembly										
W	2	top and bottom	cherry	¼	(6)	6	(152)	18⁷⁄₁₆	(468)	
X	7	dividers	cherry	¼	(6)	6	(152)	5¾	(146)	grain runs vertically
Y	2	cleats	cherry	¼	(6)	2	(51)	6	(152)	
Z	2	pencil holders	cherry	¾	(19)	1	(25)	6	(152)	
Doors										
AA	2	drop-top stiles	cherry	¾	(19)	2¼	(57)	13⅞	(352)	¾" (19mm) tbe
BB	2	drop-top rails	cherry	¾	(19)	2¼	(57)	18⅜	(467)	
CC	2	drop-top panel	cherry	¾	(19)	13⅝	(346)	15⅜	(391)	
DD	2	bottom-door stiles	cherry	¾	(19)	2¼	(57)	18⅛	(460)	
EE	2	bottom-door rails	cherry	¾	(19)	2¼	(57)	15⅜	(391)	¾" (19mm) tbe
FF	1	bottom-door panel	cherry	½	(13)	15⅝	(384)	15⅛	(384)	
GG	2	tall-door stiles	cherry	¾	(19)	2¼	(57)	51¾	(1314)	
HH	2	tall-door rails	cherry	¾	(19)	2¼	(57)	15⅜	(391)	¾" (19mm) tbe
Mirror Frame										
JJ	2	stiles	cherry	¾	(19)	2	(51)	16	(406)	
KK	1	rail	cherry	¾	(19)	2	(51)	19	(483)	
LL	1	crest rail	cherry	¾	(19)	4¼	(108)	16	(406)	

HARDWARE & SUPPLIES

- 5—2½" (65mm) × 1½" (40mm) brass ball end hinges
- 3—door handles
- 2—brass stays
- 2—brass butler-tray hinges
- 3—magnetic catches
- 16—5mm shelf pins

Construction Notes

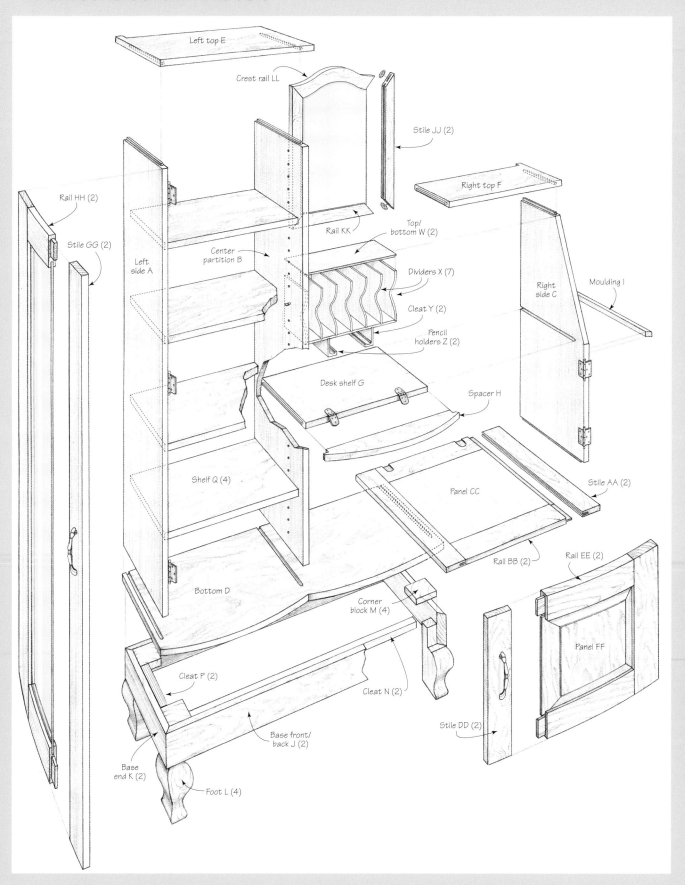

Left top E

Crest rail LL

Stile JJ (2)

Rail HH (2)

Right top F

Stile GG (2)

Rail KK

Top/ bottom W (2)

Left side A

Center partition B

Right side C

Dividers X (7)

Moulding I

Cleat Y (2)

Pencil holders Z (2)

Desk shelf G

Spacer H

Shelf Q (4)

Panel CC

Stile AA (2)

Rail BB (2)

Rail EE (2)

Bottom D

Corner block M (4)

Panel FF

Cleat P (2)

Cleat N (2)

Base front/ back J (2)

Stile DD (2)

Base end K (2)

Foot L (4)

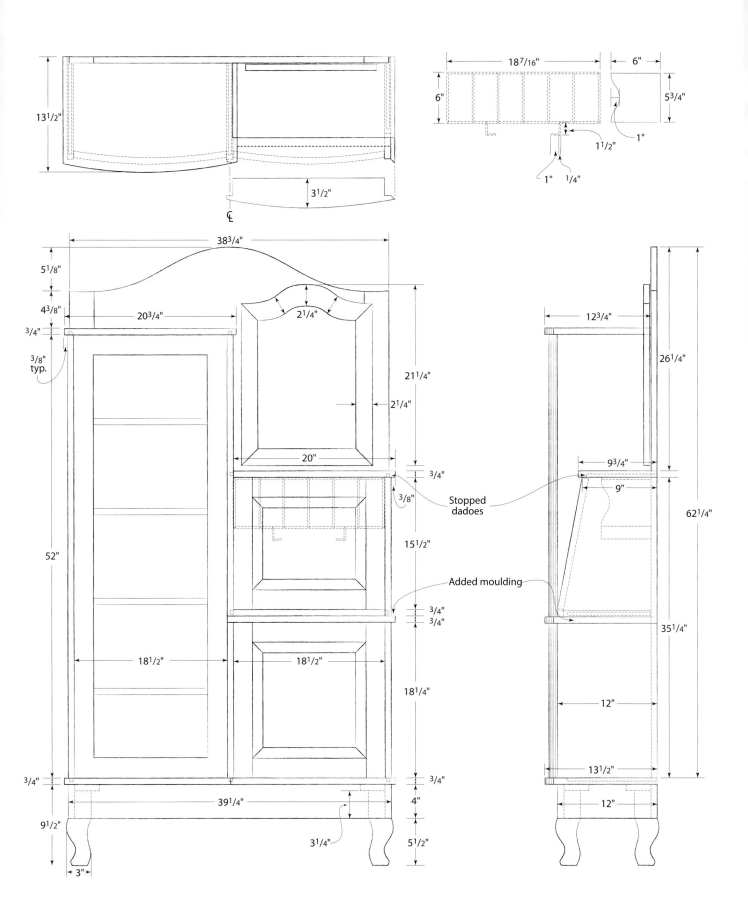

13 1/2"

18 7/16"   6"

6"   5 3/4"

1 1/2"   1"

1"   1/4"

3 1/2"

₵L

38 3/4"

5 1/8"

4 3/8"

3/4"

3/8" typ.

20 3/4"

2 1/4"

2 1/4"

21 1/4"

2 1/4"

20"

3/4"

3/8"

12 3/4"

26 1/4"

9 3/4"

9"

Stopped dadoes

62 1/4"

15 1/2"

Added moulding

52"

18 1/2"

18 1/2"

3/4"

3/4"

35 1/4"

18 1/4"

12"

3/4"

3/4"

3/4"

13 1/2"

39 1/4"

4"

9 1/2"

3 1/4"

5 1/2"

12"

3"

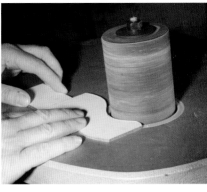

STEP 1 I cut the bottom to size and drew the full-scale plans on it. Include as many details as possible—where the partitions, sides, doors and back are located and what type of joinery will be used. As I was building the cabinet, I used this drawing as my template for all the other parts. There's nothing as frustrating as miscut parts, dadoes or tenons located in the wrong place. A clear layout will save time, material, lots of yelling, sanity and a big head-ache. Yeah, it's that important to make these drawings correct.

STEP 2 After the drawing is made and you understand how the project is to be assembled, cut out the aprons for the base. Miter the corners, apply glue to the miters and use band clamps to hold the assembly together while the glue dries. Never fear, the glued butt joints will be ok. As shown later, the legs and the corner blocks will make this base strong enough to support dancing elephants.

STEP 3 While the base apron assembly is drying, make a pattern for the feet. I used ⅛" hardboard, but stiff cardboard will also work. The pattern doesn't need to be perfect, it just needs to be a pleasing shape with smooth lines. You're going to use this to trace the profile on the foot blanks.

STEP 4 Mill the foot blanks square and cut them to length. Set the table saw's fence to 3¼" (including the width of the saw blade) and the blade height to ¾". Make a cut, as shown in the photo on two adjacent sides of each foot blank. You're on your way to creating tenons on the feet.

STEP 5 Set the band saw's fence to 2¼" and make the two long tenon cuts, stopping at the table saw cut, to create a tenon on each foot. If you don't trust yourself to stop cutting at the table saw cut, use wood scrap as a stop block. (It's obvious I don't trust myself.)

STEP 6 Now for some fun. Get the pattern you made in Step 3, grab a pencil and trace the foot profile on the outside of each foot. Make the cut as shown. Then trace the profile on the side with the cut you just made. Now make this second cut.

STEP 7 Reverse the pattern and trace the profile on the inside of the feet. Make that cut, then trace the profile on this cut and make the final profile cut as shown above. The cuts are safe to make because the feet are supported at two points on the band saw table.

STEP 8 Sand the feet until they're smooth with a nice flow to the lines of the profile. An ocillating spindle sander is the tool of choice for this type of sanding but a cut off broom handle with sandpaper wrapped around it will also work. Trust me, it's been done before.

STEP 9 Cut the corner blocks and glue them in place. Then flip the apron assembly over, put glue on the top and both sides of each foot tenon and glue the feet into place. Clamp from both sides of each foot. Clamping downward is optional but I wanted to be sure each foot was firmly held in place.

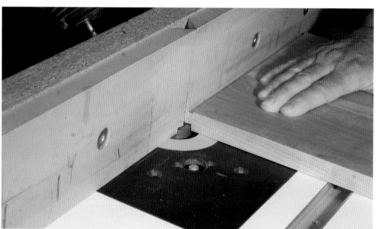

STEP 10 Double, no, triple check the cutting list, then cut out the sides, shelves and tops. (If you're using plywood, this is easy. If you're using hardwood, you may need to glue parts to width.) Also, if you're using biscuit joinery, ignore this stuff about cutting mortises and tenons. Ok, here's the stuff about cutting the mortises. Carefully layout the mortises (measure thrice, cut once), make a jig (½" or ¾" MDF) like the one in the photo. It guides the router while ploughing the mortise.

STEP 11 The tenons on the parts can be cut using the table saw or a router table. I used a rabbeting bit for making these cuts. Cut one side of the part, flip it over and cut the other side. Use some scrap wood the same thickness as your parts to setup the cuts so the tenon is the correct width. Trim the tenons at the front edges of the parts where they meet the stopped mortises. Triple check everything for fit, then assemble the cabinet. Refer to the illustrations as often as needed so you don't mess up.

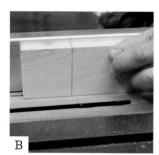
A   B

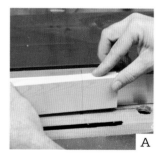
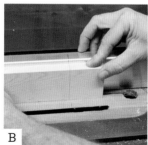
A   B

STEP 12 After cutting the grooves in the back and drop-front panel parts, I mark the center location of the table saw blade (Photo a). (When the blade is raised, this is the highest point of the blade above the table.) Then I raise the blade to the required depth of the mortises. Half of the mortises are cut

straight into the parts (Photo b), half are plunge cuts (Photo c and d). Stop the cuts when the blade centerline mark and the rail location marks line up. The back of the saw blade will cut past the mortise locations but it's OK. The panels will cover these slightly deeper cuts.

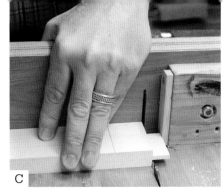

A   B   C

STEP 13 To cut the tenons on the rails, set the table saw's fence (including the blade thickness) to the length of the tenon and set the blade height to about one-third of the thickness of the rails (Photo a). Use test pieces to fine-tune the setup. Then nibble away the material to create the tenons (Photos b and c). Panels will cover these slightly deeper cuts.

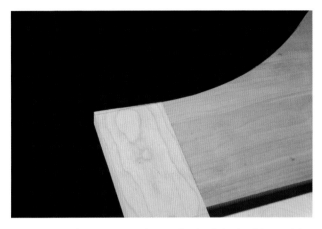

STEP 14 To assemble the back, apply glue only at the stile-and-rail joints. Then put the center stile in place on each rail, slide the panels in place and attache the outside stiles. Put a clamp across each rail and one from top to bottom to pull the joints together.

STEP 15 I drew a square line on both of the back's outside stiles where they meet the crest rail. This line guided me as I blended the crest rail curve into the tops of the stiles. When all the cabinet parts have been cut and dry-fitted, it's time to assemble the cabinet. Use the illustrations to help you put things together properly.

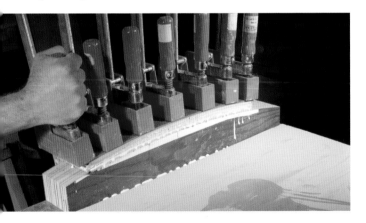

STEP 16 I prefer laminated bending over steam bending because the results can be predicted. The springback of laminated parts is zero, whereas steam-bent parts tend to straighten a little when they're taken from the mold and that springback can't be determined with much accuracy. The radius of the bend will de-termine the thickness of the laminations, which will result in zero springback if the laminations are the correct thickness. For this project, ⅛"-thick laminations were perfect. Determine the radius for the door rails by referencing your full-scale drawing. Make a gluing jig to this radius, wax the curved surface of the jig so the glue won't stick to it and make the door rails. Let each rail sit 24 hours in the jig

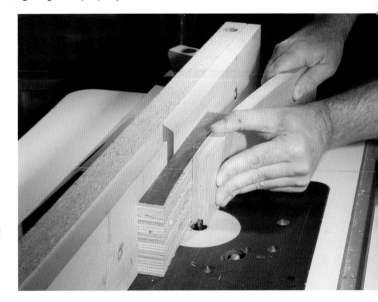

STEP 17 Use the scrap from making the rail-gluing jig as a guide for routing the groove in the center of the curved door rails. Make a shallow pass, then raise the bit and make another pass. Do this until you reach the proper groove depth. Use this same router bit to cut the grooves in the door stiles.

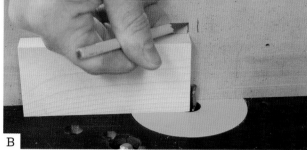

A   B

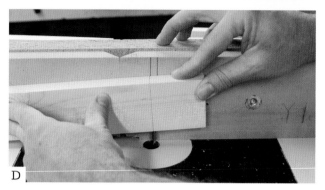

C   D

STEP 18 I used the router table to cut the grooves in the curved-doors' parts. After cutting the grooves in the parts, raise the bit to the depth of the mortises. On the router table fence, mark both sides of the router bit (Photos a and b).

Use the right hand mark as the stopping point for the straight-in cuts (Photo c) and the left hand mark for the start of the plunge cuts (Photo d).

STEP 19 Cut the curved rails to length. Reference your full-scale drawing to determine the angle of the cut. At the ends of each rail, the cut should be 90 degrees to the curve. Of course, this isn't really true, but visualize about 1" (25mm) of the ends of the rails and pretend that that part is straight and gauge your cut from it.

STEP 20 Use a tenoning fixture with a wedge attached to it to hold the rails so their cut ends rest flat on the top of the table saw. Set up the fixture and cut the tenons so they fit snugly into the grooves in the stiles. Assemble the glass door frame. Then use a rabbeting bit to cut the rabbets for the glass. The router will sit flat enough on the curved rails. You'll need to square the corners of the rabbets with a chisel. See suppliers list for ordering curved glass.

STEP 21 I used 5 boards to make the curved door panel. Using more boards means less work to create the curve. The outside of the panel has a 54" radius. The panel uses 16.2° of the circumference of the circle. Divide that by 5. The angle of each edge-to-edge joint is 3.25°. Divide that by 2. The miter cut is 1.62°—give or take a little. Make slight adjustments as needed to make the required radius. When the door panel dry-fits to the correct curve, lay the parts face up, tape the joints, turn the assembly over, apply glue in the bevel joints and fold them together. Use gentle clamping pressure to hold the panel until the glue cures (24 hours).

STEP 22 To start creating the curve on the panel, break out your handplane and level the joints until they start blending with the flat surfaces of the boards.

STEP 23 This is the best way to true the curve: use an 80-grit sanding belt wrapped around a wood block and sand across the wood grain. Then use a random orbital sander to clean it up.

STEP 24 Use a curved scraper to roughout the curve on the inside of the panel. Finish up with the random orbital sander.

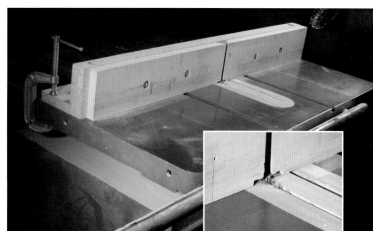

STEP 25 My good friend, the late Danny Proulx, showed me this method of cutting raised panels using the table saw. Set up a fence centered on (front to back) and at a right angle to the blade (I used the fence from my router table). Use a carbide-tipped saw blade and raise it ⅛". Do not try to cut any deeper at anytime.

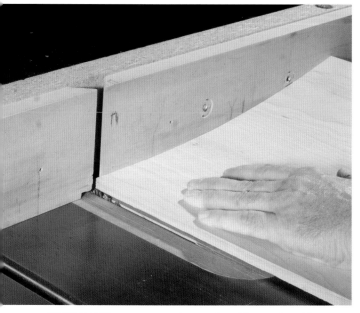

STEP 26 The great part about using this panel-making method is that it works for making the curved raised panel.

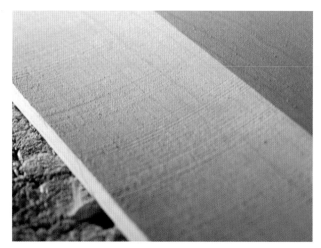

STEP 27 The slower you feed the panel past the saw blade, the smoother the cut. Cleanup the cuts using a scraper and sandpaper.

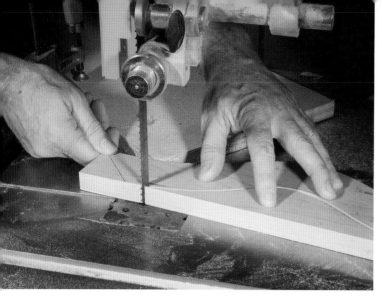

STEP 28 Lay out the shape of the mirror-frame top rail and cut it.

STEP 29 Sand the curves of the rail smooth. Then use a rabbeting bit to cut rabbets in the mirror frame's parts.

STEP 30 Cut the miters on the mirror frame parts, cut a slot in the miters for a No.1 biscuit and assemble the frame using a band clamp. Check the frame for squareness and let the glue dry. Make a template for the mirror, take it to your local hardware store and have them cut you a mirror. The hardware store folks like it when I come in with something out of the ordinary and I like the personal attention (which I usually don't get at a large chain homebuilding center).

STEP 31 I've been installing butt hinges for years using jigs just like this one. They're easy to make and do the job quickly and accurately. Cut the mortise 1/16" less that the thickness of the closed hinge. When the hinge is installed, this will automatically create the spacing between the hinge side of the door and the cabinet. See photo 32. Square the corners of the mortise.

STEP 32 Install the butt hinges on the door. Then draw a line where the screws of the hinges will be located on the inside of the cabinet. Rest the door on a spacer on the bottom of the cabinet and drill one pilot hole at the top hinge. Install the screw and gently close the door to check its alignment to the face of the cabinet. Note any door in-or-out adjustments that need to be made. Open the door and install a screw in the bottom hinge, accounting for the adjustment if necessary. Repeat the closing and checking of the door's alignment. When all is to your liking, install the remaining screws.

STEP 33 I made a jig for cutting the mortises for the drop-leaf desktop. Note the blue tape used to fine tune the fit of the mortise to the hinge plate exactly.

STEP 34 When the desk is opened, your eye is immediately drawn to the bright brass hinges, so make them a good fit. The drop-front desktop and the shelf it's hinged to need to be flush when the desktop is open. The butler tray hinges look good and work perfectly. The installation of the hinges is just like the butt hinge installation. Install the hinges on the desktop first, then attach them to the shelf.

STEP 35 After the cabinet is completely assembled, add this filler on the tops. It "wraps" the top around the back and closes the gap between the two. You could attach these fillers before you install the tops but it's a fragile assembly at best.

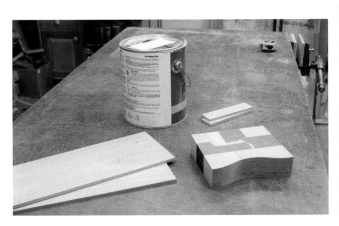

STEP 36 Cut the parts for the cubby holes. Stack and tape the vertical dividers together. Draw a curve on the front edges (I used the bottom of the paint can in the photo as my template) and cut the whole mess in one shot on the band saw. Then sand them, blending the curve with a slight radius to make a pleasing shape.

STEP 37 I cut the dadoes for the vertical cubby hole dividers using a router table. The table saw will work equally as well.

STEP 38 I used a mutiprofile router bit to make the pencil holders. Make one long piece, glue the bracket to it and cut the lengths required. The cubby assembly is nailed together. Predrill for the nails so the vertical dividers don't split.

STEP 39 After finish-sanding the entire project, I used a paintbrush to apply ammonia to the raw wood. (The left side of the wood sample in the photo shows how the ammonia affects the cherry.) After the ammonia dried, I sanded the raised grain and applied a coat of catalyzed lacquer. When the lacquer was dry, I sanded the finish using 220-grit sandpaper. I applied two additional coats of lacquer and allowed them to cure for one week, then used No.0000 steel wool to rub the finish. To make the finish a little shinier, I applied a coat of wax.

cutting list

No.	Item	Dimensions T W L	Material
1	Back	$^3/_8$" x 3$^1/_2$" x 12"	Pine
2	Sides	$^3/_8$" x 2$^1/_2$" x 10$^3/_8$"	Pine
1	Front	$^3/_8$" x 2$^3/_4$" x 8$^1/_4$"	Pine
1	Divider	$^3/_8$" x 2$^1/_8$" x 2$^3/_4$"	Pine
1	Bottom	$^3/_8$" x 2$^1/_2$" x 2$^3/_4$"	Pine
1	Drawer front	$^3/_8$" x 1$^3/_4$" x 2$^3/_4$"	Pine
2	Drawer sides	$^1/_4$" x 1$^3/_4$" x 2$^3/_8$"	Pine
1	Drawer back	$^1/_4$" x 1$^3/_4$" x 2$^1/_4$"	Pine
1	Drawer bottom	$^1/_4$" x 2$^1/_4$" x 2$^1/_2$"	Plywood

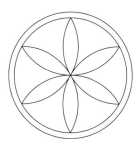

Enlarge 200% for full-size decorative design pattern.

Roadhouse Pipe Box

by Jim Stuard

Back in the days of horse and buggy, travelers would stop at a roadhouse, where they'd likely see a box like this on the wall. It held a selection of clay pipes for the use of patrons. A traveler who wanted a smoke would take a pipe from the box and break off a short piece of the stem as a sanitary measure. After use, the pipe was put back in the box for the next smoker. This accounts for the unusually long stems on clay pipes.

If you don't smoke, you could always use this box to hold dried flowers or other decorative items.

Construction is simple. The front, divider and bottom are captured between the sides and attached with glue and nails. That assembly is then glued and nailed to the back. Begin by cutting out all the pieces according to the sizes in the Schedule of Materials. Glue and nail the divider perpendicular and flush to the bottom of the front.

Now glue and nail the sides to the front, flush to the top of the front. Glue and nail the bottom in place.

Cut a radius on the back according to the diagram, then drill a ½" hole for hanging on the wall. Before attaching the back, paint the inside of the box. Mask the edges of the back where the sides meet and paint it also. After the paint dries, remove the tape from the back and glue and nail the back to the box assembly.

The drawer is tricky only in that it is so small. Before assembly, cut a ¼" × ⅛" rabbet on one edge of all four drawer sides. This will capture the bottom. Cut a ¼" × ¼" rabbet into three edges of the front. Nail the sides into this rabbet. Nail the back between the sides and nail the bottom into the rabbet on the bottom edges.

After fitting the drawer to the opening, sand and paint all the parts. Lay out the decorative design using the pattern and a compass. Use a contrasting paint to highlight the design. Attach a screw-in pull on the drawer front and you are ready for the next wayfarer that stops by.

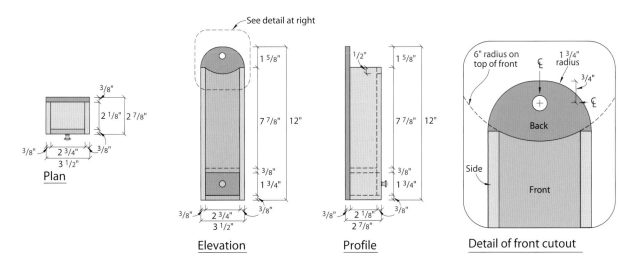

Plan

Elevation

Profile

Detail of front cutout

Country Dry Sink

by Troy Sexton

Though this dry sink won't store pitchers of milk fresh from the cow, it will give your kitchen an old-time feel that no modern cabinet could. that when the glue finally gives way, as it will someday, it's the nails that will hold the piece together.

Now nail the nailing strip between the sides. The nailing strip should be flush to the top of the sides and ½" in from the back edge of the sides. You'll nail your back to this when the project is complete.

To complete the lower case, glue and nail the face frame to the case. When the glue is dry, cut the shape of the base on the front and sides using a jigsaw. Then clean up your cuts using sandpaper. Now it's time to move on to the top.

Make the Top to Last

There's some cross-grain construction in the top, so you need to be careful about how you put it together to ensure the top doesn't self-destruct.

Begin by gluing up the boards for the top piece, cutting the top to finished size and sanding it to its final grit. Cut a ¼" x ¼" chamfer on the top edge to soften the edge.

Cut your three splash pieces to size and cut the curved parts. The back splash gets a 3" radius cut on either end. And the side splashes get a 1" radius cut on the front edge as shown in the drawings. Finish sand all the pieces and follow the instructions under the photos.

Finishing Touches

I make the drawers using half-blind dovetails. I build a simple jig that cranks these out in just a few minutes.

To keep the drawers running straight, I nailed in ¾" x 1" strips of wood on the upper fixed shelf and stops at the back of the case to keep the drawer fronts flush to the front of the case.

Troy Sexton designs and builds custom furniture in Sunbury, Ohio, for his company, Sexton Classic American Furniture. Troy was a contributing editor for *Popular Woodworking*.

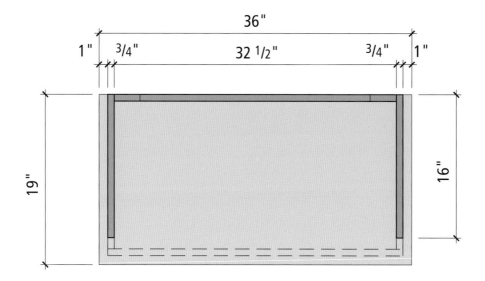

Plan

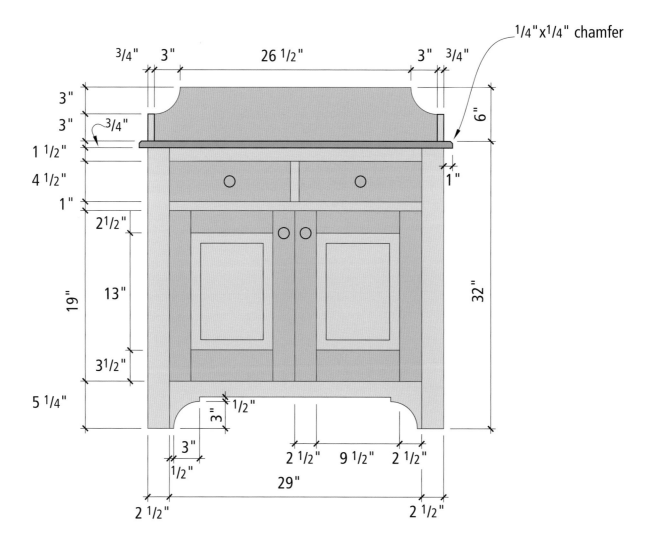

¹/4"x¹/4" chamfer

Elevation

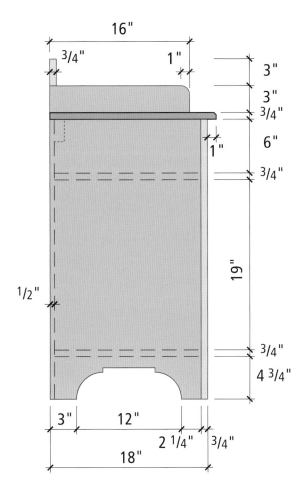

16"

3/4" 1"

3"
3"
3/4"
1"
6"
3/4"

19"

1/2"

3/4"
4 3/4"

3" 12"
2 1/4" 3/4"
18"

Profile

NO.	ITEM	DIMENSIONS (INCHES) T	W	L	MATERIAL	NOTES
Face Frame						
❏ 2	Stiles	³/₄	2¹/₂	31¹/₄	Maple	
❏ 1	Top rail	³/₄	1¹/₂	31	Maple	1" TBE
❏ 1	Bottom rail	³/₄	5¹/₄	31	Maple	1" TBE
❏ 1	Mid-stile	³/₄	1	6¹/₂	Maple	1" TBE
❏ 1	Mid-rail	³/₄	1	31	Maple	1" TBE
Case						
❏ 2	Sides	³/₄	17¹/₄	31¹/₄	Maple	
❏ 2	Fixed shelves	³/₄	16³/₄	33	Maple	
❏	Back	¹/₂	33	31¹/₄	Poplar	shiplapped
❏ 1	Top	³/₄	19	36	Maple	
❏ 1	Splash, back	³/₄	6	32¹/₂	Maple	3" radius
❏ 2	Splash, sides	³/₄	3	16	Maple	1" radius
❏ 1	Nailing strip	³/₄	1¹/₂	32¹/₂	Poplar	
Doors						
❏ 4	Stiles	³/₄	2¹/₂	19	Maple	
❏ 2	Top rails	³/₄	2¹/₂	11¹/₂	Maple	1" TBE
❏ 2	Bottom rails	³/₄	3¹/₂	11¹/₂	Maple	1" TBE
❏ 2	Panels	⁵/₈	10	14	Maple	
Drawers						
❏ 2	Fronts	³/₄	4³/₈	13⁷/₈	Maple	
❏ 4	Sides	¹/₂	4³/₈	17	Poplar	
❏ 2	Backs	¹/₂	3¹/₂	13⁷/₈	Poplar	
❏ 2	Bottoms	¹/₂	16	13³/₈	Poplar	

TBE = TENON ON BOTH ENDS

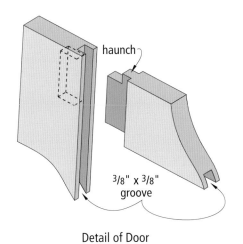

haunch

3/8" x 3/8"
groove

Detail of Door
Joinery

Sources

Horton Brasses Inc.
800-754-9127
www.horton-brasses.com
1¹/₄" knobs (4)
Woodworker's Supply
800-645-9292
www.woodworker.com
Amerock adjustable
hinges (4)
item #891-749,
$4.49 each

The back is made from ¹/₂"-thick poplar boards that I shiplap so the edges overlap. I also cut a bead on the shiplapped edges using a beading bit in my router. Fit the back Traditional American dry sinks were made from yellow pine and had deep wooden troughs on top that were useful for storing pitchers, churns and buckets of liquids. Now that we've got refrigerators and ice makers, the dry sink has graduated to become an expensive item at antique markets.

This updated version preserves the form of the traditional dry sink, with its high splash guard on back and

Begin building the top by gluing and nailing the side splash pieces to the back splash pieces. I like to hold the back splash in place using a vise to keep everything in line as it's nailed together.

Now glue and nail the splash pieces to the top. Turn the splash upside-down and put a bead of glue on the entire length of the back splash. Then put a bead of glue on the back third of the side splash. If you glue the entire side splash, your top might bust apart after a few seasons.

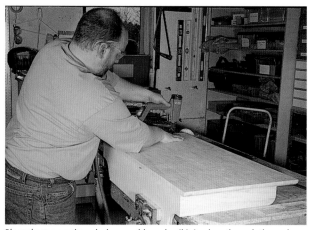

Place the top on the splash assembly and nail it in place through the underside of the top.

storage down below, but I've altered a few key components. Instead of a sunken wooden trough on top, I've added two drawers. And instead of yellow pine, this dry sink is made from curly maple. Put the finished project in your kitchen to add a country touch to a farm home, or use it as a buffet in an informal dining room.

Traditional Construction

I build all my casework the same way, and I'm convinced that these methods will ensure that the furniture will be around for a long time. Begin by building the face frame of the cabinet because most of the cabinet dimensions are based on the face frame. I use mortise-and-tenon joinery to join the rails and stiles. I make the tenons on all the rails 1" long, and all the mortises 1⅟₁₆" deep, which will ensure your tenons won't bottom out in your mortises and give some space for excess glue to go. Dry-fit the face-frame parts, then put glue in the mortises and glue up all the rails and stiles. Start with the center rail and stile and work out.

Doors Next

Once the glue is dry from the face frame, I like to make my doors because they are easier to hang and fit while the face frame can be laid flat on my bench. The doors are built much the same way as the face frame, with 1"-long tenons on the rails. To hold the panel in place, I plow a ⅜" x ⅜" groove down the inside edge of all the door parts. Be sure to make the tenons on the rails haunched because of this groove.

Once you have the rails and stiles fit, measure the opening for the panel and cut your stock to size, making sure that you leave a ⅛" gap all around to accommodate wood movement in the panel. I cut an 8° bevel on the edges of the panel using my shaper, though you can easily cut this bevel by tilting the blade about 12° on your table saw. Finish sand the panel and add one coat of stain.

Place the panel in the groove, glue up the mortise-and-tenon joints and clamp the doors. You'll notice that I make the doors the same size as my opening in the face frame. This is on purpose. Once my doors are complete, I trim them to size on my jointer. Hang the doors in the face frame, then remove the doors and move onto the case.

Build the Case

Begin building the case by gluing up some boards to make the side pieces and shelves. Once those are cut to finished size, cut ¾"-wide x ¼"-deep dadoes to hold the two fixed shelves in place.

The bottom dado is located 4¾" from the bottom edge of sides. This will make the bottom shelf stick up ¼" above the bottom rail of the face frame and serve as a door stop. The second dado should be flush to the top of the center rail because the drawers will ride on that shelf. Now cut ½" x ¼" rabbets in the sides for the back.

Put a bead of glue in the dadoes, then put the shelves in the dadoes and nail the case together through the sides. Some people might wince at nailing a case together this way; I don't. I figure that when the glue finally gives way, as it will someday, it's the nails that will hold the piece together.

Now nail the nailing strip between the sides. The nailing strip should be flush to the top of the sides and ½" in from the back edge of the sides. You'll nail your back to this when the project is complete.

To complete the lower case, glue and nail the face frame to the case. When the glue is dry, cut the shape of the base on the front and sides using a jigsaw. Then clean up your cuts using sandpaper. Now it's time to move on to the top.

Make the Top to Last

There's some cross-grain construction in the top, so you need to be careful about how you put it together to ensure the top doesn't self-destruct.

Begin by gluing up the boards for the top piece, cutting the top to finished size and sanding it to its final grit. Cut a ¼" x ¼" chamfer on the top edge to soften the edge.

Cut your three splash pieces to size and cut the curved parts. The back splash gets a 3" radius cut on either end. And the side splashes get a 1" radius cut on the front edge as shown in the drawings. Finish sand all the pieces and follow the instructions under the photos.

Finishing Touches

I make the drawers using half-blind dovetails. I build a simple jig that cranks these out in just a few minutes. To keep the drawers running straight, I nailed in ¾" x 1" strips of wood on the upper fixed shelf and stops at the back of the case to keep the drawer fronts

flush to the front of the case.

The back is made from ½"-thick poplar boards that I shiplap so the edges overlap. I also cut a bead on the shiplapped edges using a beading bit in my router. Fit the back pieces, being sure to leave a gap between each board; don't nail them in place until the dry sink is finished.

Now finish sand all the parts, putty your nail holes and dye the project. I use a diluted red aniline dye, followed by three coats of lacquer.

Now put a bead of glue on the side pieces and top rail of the face frame. The sides will expand and contract the same as the sides pieces so there isn't a cross-grain problem here. Toenail the top into the case piece.

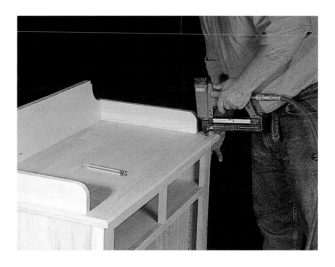

Blanket Chest

by John McGuane

Placed at the foot of a bed, this cedar blanket chest is perfect for extra storage and can double as a bench. The natural moth-repellent properties of the aromatic cedar will protect your blankets, sweaters and fine woolens for years to come.

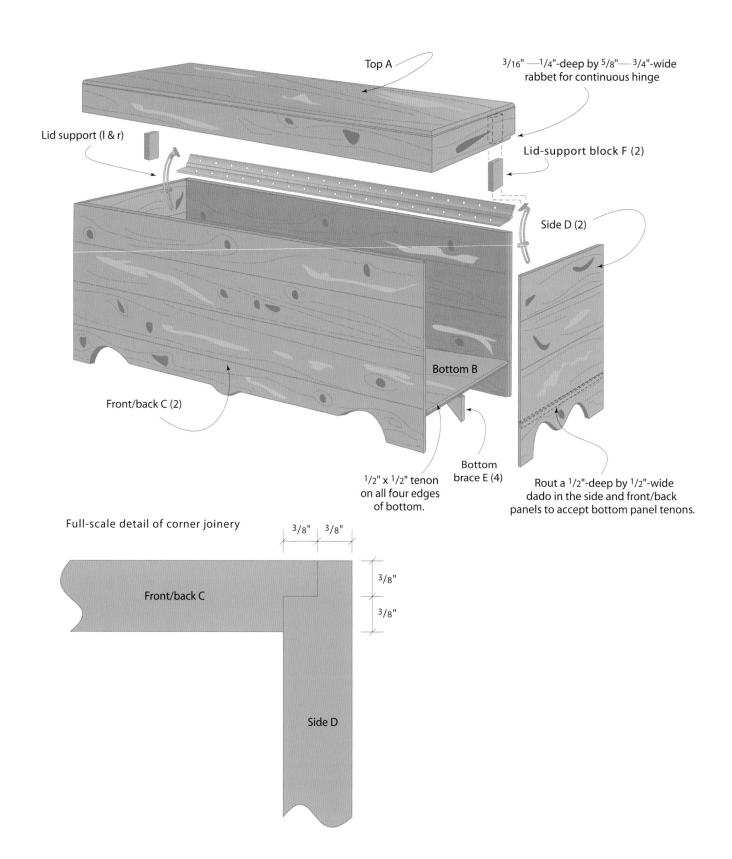

Top A

3/16"—1/4"-deep by 5/8"—3/4"-wide rabbet for continuous hinge

Lid support (l & r)

Lid-support block F (2)

Side D (2)

Front/back C (2)

Bottom B

1/2" x 1/2" tenon on all four edges of bottom.

Bottom brace E (4)

Rout a 1/2"-deep by 1/2"-wide dado in the side and front/back panels to accept bottom panel tenons.

Full-scale detail of corner joinery

3/8"   3/8"

3/8"

3/8"

Front/back C

Side D

cutting list

INCHES (MILLIMETERS)

REFERENCE	QUANTITY	PART	STOCK	THICKNESS	(mm)	WIDTH	(mm)	LENGTH	(mm)
A	1	top	aromatic cedar	3/4	(19)	18	(457)	44	(1118)
B	1	bottom	aromatic cedar	3/4	(19)	17 1/4	(438)	43 1/4	(1099)
C	2	front/back	aromatic cedar	3/4	(19)	23	(584)	44	(1118)
D	2	sides	aromatic cedar	3/4	(19)	23	(584)	18	(457)
E	4	bottom braces	aromatic cedar	3/4	(19)	3	(76)	3	(76)
F	2	lid-support blocks	aromatic cedar	3/4	(19)	2	(51)	4	(102)

HARDWARE & SUPPLIES

1	44" (1118mm) brass-plated steel continuous hinge
2	friction lid supports (left and right)
10-20	No. 20 biscuits
a few	4d finishing nails

APRON PATTERNS

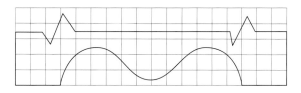

18"

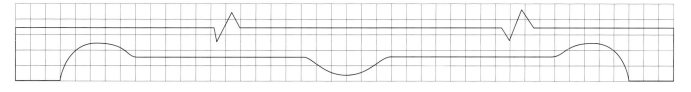

44"

Each square represents 1".

STEP 1 Aromatic cedar has a busy grain pattern. You can cut the wood to suit your personal taste. The light-colored sapwood contrasts dramatically with the heartwood. If you want to get good yield from the lumber, try different configurations of the boards until you're satisfied with the overall pattern.

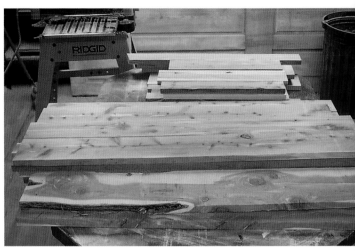

STEP 2 One benefit of using aromatic cedar is that your shop will smell wonderful for days. Plane the lumber and cut it so several of the knots remain. The knots contain a lot of resin, which adds to the aroma.

STEP 3 Use biscuits to reinforce the edge joints. Mark the location of the biscuits about one per foot. Be careful where you place the biscuits so they aren't located in the middle of a cut.

STEP 4 Be sure the panels remain flat at glue-up time. After the glue dries, cut the panels to size.

STEP 5 The corner joints of this box use a double-rabbeted joint. I cut the 3/8" × 3/8" rabbets in the front/back and side panels, using a straight-cutting bit in a router mounted under a table.

STEP 6 Use a pair of outfeed rollers and a board as an extra pair of hands to keep the workpiece level.

STEP 7 Reset your router table fence and cut the 1/2" × 1/2" dadoes in the front/back and side panels for the bottom panel.

STEP 8 Dry fit all the parts before final glue-up. This gives you a chance to rehearse the steps for glue-up.

STEP 9 Use the provided apron patterns and a jigsaw to cut decorative curves in the bottom of the vertical panels. These cutouts are more than embellishments. They create four feet that will allow the box sit level on uneven floors.

STEP 10 Using the front panel as a template, transfer the decorative design to the back panel. The side panels use a variation of the pattern used on the front/back panels. Then, rout the ½" × ½" groove for the bottom panel into the side panels and the front/back panels.

STEP 11 Cut the ½" × ½" tenon on the edges of the bottom panel using a jointer or a straight-cutting bit in the router. This tenon will fit into the grooves that were routed in step 10.

STEP 12 Do another dry fit with the bottom included.

STEP 13 First, rip 4" from the top of the side and front/back panels. These pieces will be used for the sides of the lid. Then apply glue and assemble the chest.

STEP 14 Using the assembled chest as a gluing template, glue the sides of the lid together. Use waxed paper between the chest and lid at the joints so the glue won't attach the lid sides to the chest.

STEP 15 Glue the top to the lid sides. If necessary, use a few small nails to hold the lid in place while you clamp it. The nail holes can be filled later.

STEP 16 Use a sanding drum attached to a hand drill to smooth
the curved edges of the box.

STEP 17 Rout a decorative profile on the edges of the top and
on the curved detail along the bottom of the box.

STEP 18 Cut the rabbet in the back, bottom edge of the lid, using a jointer or router. The depth of the rabbet should be the same as the thickness of the closed hinge. Cut the continuous hinge to length and attach it to the lid, then attach the lid to the chest. Glue the lid-support blocks in place, then install the lid supports. Finally, glue the bottom braces in place.

STEP 19 To prepare the chest for finishing, tape the edges of the lid and box to stop the finish from bleeding into the chest. The inside of the chest is left unfinished and can be sanded periodically in coming years to release more moth-repellent scent.

STEP 20 Seal the entire exterior of the box with two coats of lacquer. Then apply two layers of spar varnish, sanding lightly between coats.

Burlington Farmers Desk

This primitive and unusual lift-lid desk proves
that pine and nails can go a long way.

by Christopher Schwarz

It was hotter than two rats fighting in a wool sock when Senior Editor David Thiel and I were scouring an antiques show in Burlington, Kentucky, for ideas and old tools. We were buying some lemonade (which, ounce for ounce, was more expensive than premium gasoline) when Dave saw this desk sitting behind an old truck. We should have risked the wrath of our wives and bought it, but instead we made a rough sketch that became the desk you see here.

It's doubtful the person who built the original was more than a casual woodworker, because he or she hadn't accounted for wood movement at all. True, the desk had survived — despite its cross-grain construction problems — but we felt compelled to remedy some of its wood movement troubles when we built this reproduction. However, I just had to bite my lip and hope for the best when I nailed the moulding to the end grain on the top pieces. You could get around this problem with a sliding dovetail, but that seemed silly for a primitive piece.

Construction is mostly nails and glue, although the box is made using finger joints. Then you nail in a plywood bottom and nail the legs into notches cut in the corners of the plywood. The fixed part of the top is nailed and glued to the box. The hinged top is nailed, glued and reinforced with braces to the angled front piece. Nail in some dividers, build some drawers and you're done.

Begin construction by cutting all the pieces to size according to the Schedule of Materials. Cut the two tapers on each leg according to the diagram; use a tapering jig on your table saw or cut them on a band saw and clean up the cut on a jointer. Now cut the ½"-wide finger joints for the box on your table saw. (See the article "Benjamin Seaton's Tool Chest" in the September 1998 issue of *Popular Woodworking Magazine* to learn how to make a jig to do this. Back issues are available on our Web site at www.popwood.com.) Cut the angled front out of the front piece with your jigsaw or band saw.

Now fit the bottom. I used knotty pine plywood. Beware: It's so expensive (about $60 for a 4x8 sheet) you'll feel like you've been beaten like a tied-up goat. So you might want to buy a decent grade of construction plywood from the home center

What's "Glaze"? Where Can I Get it?

Because oil finishes reign supreme in many home shops and catalogs (unfortunately), an often over-looked finishing tool is glaze. What's glaze? It's a really thick stain or a thinned paint that you apply between layers of clear finish. Glaze is used by many professional finishers to add depth to the wood or to even out the color among different-looking boards in their furniture. Plus, it's great for creating an antiqued look. Here are two sources for glaze:

1. A professional paint store. Painters use glaze all the time, so most pro paint stores carry it.

2. Merit Industries, (800) 856-4441, www.meritin-dustries.com, carries three brands of glaze at discount prices.

For more information on glazing, read Bob Flexner's *Understanding Wood Finishing* (Rodale Press).

cutting list

No.	Item	Dimensions T W L	Material
4	Legs	2½" x 2½" x 36½"	Pine
2	Front/back	¾" x 7¼" x 34½"	Pine
2	Sides	¾" x 7¼" x 30"	Pine
2	Tops	¾" x 15" x 34½"	Pine
I	Bottom*	¾" x 28½" x 33"	Pine ply.
2	Vert. dividers	¾" x 9½" x 6½"	Pine
I	Horiz. dividers	¾" x 9½" x 33"	Pine
2	Braces for front	¾" x 3" x 3"	Pine
2	Battens	¾" x 2" x 10"	Pine
3	Drawer fronts	¾" x 2¹³⁄₁₆" x 10⅜"	Scraps
6	Drawer sides	½" x 2¹³⁄₁₆" x 10"	Pine
3	Drawer backs	½" x 2⁵⁄₁₆" x 9⅞"	Pine
3	Drawer bottoms	¼" x 9⅞" x 9⅝"	Plywood
	Ogee trim	25' of ¾" x ¾"	Pine

*Size includes ¹⁄₁₆ pine edging

supplies

Van Dyke's Restorers
(800) 558-1234 www.vandykes.com
• Forged Brass Pull, #209413, $15.99
• Hinges, #AG-02265477, $7.99 a pair
• Knobs, #209406, $8.49 each

and sand the heck out of it, instead. Cut four 2½" × 2½" notches in the pine plywood's corners to make room for the legs. Glue a ¹⁄₁₆"-thick strip of pine to the front edge of the plywood to hide that edge when the desk is open. Then dry fit the four sides of the box around the bottom. When you've got a good fit, glue the finger joints together around the bottom. Clamp and allow to dry. When dry, nail the bottom in place (moulding will cover the nail holes). Now glue and nail the legs in place. Clamp and allow to dry.

Next work on the top. Cut the mortises for the two butt hinges into the edges where the two top pieces will meet. Nail and glue the fixed top in place on the back half of the desk. Install the hinges on the two top pieces. Then glue and nail the angled front flush to the front edge of the top that pivots. Cut out the triangular braces and nail them in place behind the angled front piece for extra support. When everything seems to be working, screw the two battens to the flip top to help keep the pine from warping. Be sure to make the screw holes in the batten pieces elongated ovals that run with the grain. This will allow your top to shrink and expand without snapping the screw heads.

Now turn to the desk's interior dividers. They are joined by ¾" × 4¾" lap joints so the dividers slide together and then slide in place inside the desk. Note that the vertical dividers are cut so that the grain runs from the top to the desk's bottom. This keeps you from seeing end grain on the dividers and stops the divider from eventually breaking the fixed top off your desk. Finish the inside of the desk, nail the dividers in place and then nail moulding to the two top pieces and the bottom edge of the box.

Next build your drawers. I used ¼" dovetails to join the sides to the drawer fronts. Then I cut ¼" × ½" rabbets on the back ends of the sides to hold the back piece in place. The plywood bottom is held in place in a ¼" × ¼" groove in the sides and drawer front. Glue some scraps in the box to serve as drawer stops.

To achieve the dirty-looking aged finish, first brush on one coat of orange shellac and allow it to dry. Rag on warm brown glaze, allow it to sit for about 15 or 20 minutes, and rub off most of it, except in the corners. Allow the glaze to dry overnight. Then cover the entire project with two coats of a clear finish.

Finally, cross your fingers and hope your pine is stable.

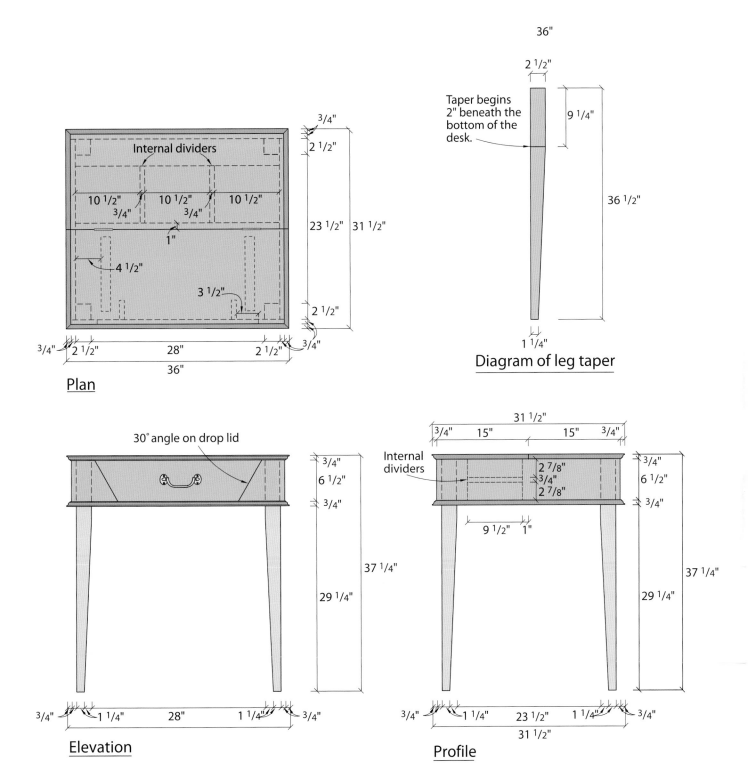

36"

2 1/2"

Taper begins 2" beneath the bottom of the desk.

9 1/4"

36 1/2"

1 1/4"

Diagram of leg taper

3/4"

2 1/2"

Internal dividers

10 1/2"   **10 1/2"**   **10 1/2"**

3/4"   **3/4"**

23 1/2"   **31 1/2"**

1"

4 1/2"

3 1/2"

2 1/2"

3/4"   **2 1/2"**   **28"**   **2 1/2"**   **3/4"**

36"

Plan

30° angle on drop lid

3/4"

6 1/2"

3/4"

37 1/4"

29 1/4"

3/4"   **1 1/4"**   **28"**   **1 1/4"**   **3/4"**

Elevation

31 1/2"

3/4"   **15"**   **15"**   **3/4"**

Internal dividers

2 7/8"
3/4"
2 7/8"

3/4"

6 1/2"

3/4"

9 1/2"   **1"**

37 1/4"

29 1/4"

3/4"   **1 1/4"**   **23 1/2"**   **1 1/4"**   **3/4"**

31 1/2"

Profile

Wastebasket

by Thane Lorbach

A simple wastebasket — not so fast! This piece is more complicated than it looks. Building this wastebasket teaches you about tapered frames and panels, how to cut parallel and opposite angles, how to resaw and bookmatch. In addition, you'll learn a simple mortise-and-tenon technique and a fast and simple way to cut miters on a jointer.

More reasons to love this project: It's small so it doesn't require a great deal of wood and requires no hardware. It's also beautiful, a little challenging and makes a great finishing touch for a home office.

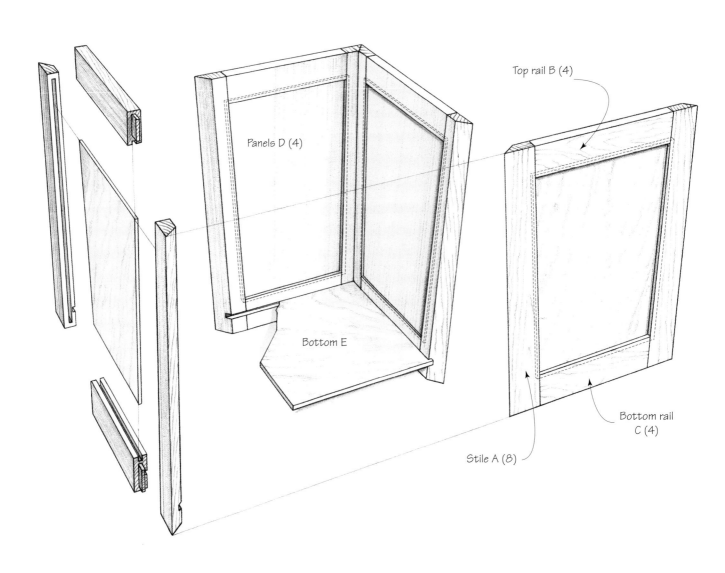

Top rail B (4)

Panels D (4)

Bottom E

Bottom rail
C (4)

Stile A (8)

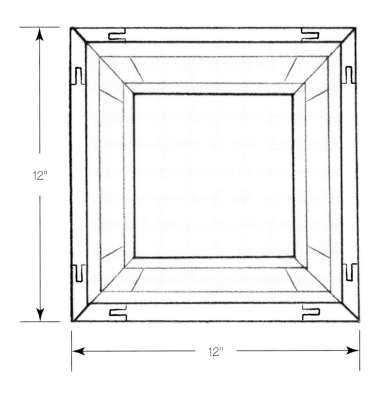

12"

12"

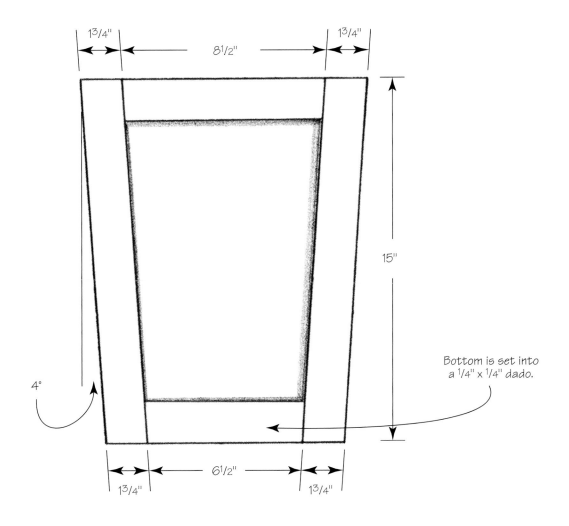

1³/4"

8¹/2"

1³/4"

15"

4°

Bottom is set into a ¹/4" x ¹/4" dado.

1³/4"

6¹/2"

1³/4"

cutting list

INCHES (MILLIMETERS)

REFERENCE	QUANTITY	PART	STOCK	THICKNESS		WIDTH		LENGTH		COMMENTS
A	8	stiles	white oak	¾	(19)	1¾	(44)	15³⁄₁₆	(386)	angled cut both ends
B	4	top rails	white oak	¾	(19)	1¾	(44)	9½	(241)	½" (13mm) tenons both ends
C	4	bottom rails	white oak	¾	(19)	1¾	(45)	7¾	(197)	
D	4	panels	white oak	¼	(6)	9	(229)	11½	(292)	
E	1	bottom	white oak	¼	(6)	9¼	(235)	9¼	(235)	

HARDWARE & SUPPLIES

- wood glue
- stain
- polyurethane finish

STEP 1 Set the miter gauge to 4° and make a cut on one end of all of the rails and stiles.

STEP 2 Leave the miter gauge at the same setting and set the fence to the stile length, then flip the stile over end for end, reference the cut end flat against the fence and make the second cut. This will make the two parallel cuts. When one end of a stile is placed flat on the table, the stile will stand at a 4° angle. Cut all eight stiles to length.

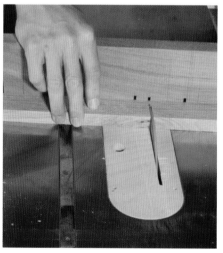

STEP 3 Set the fence for the length of the bottom rails. (Don't forget to add the length of both tenons before cutting the rails to length.) Flip the rail end for end (but not over). Note that the cut end will not sit flush against the fence, only the tip will touch the fence. Make the second cut on the four bottom rails. Reset the fence to the length of the top rails and make the cuts.

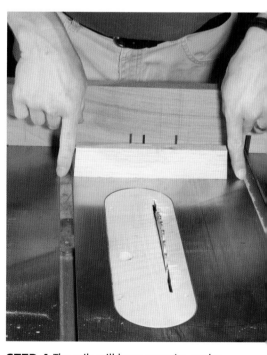

STEP 4 The rails will have opposite angles and the stiles will have parallel angles. I'm showing exaggerated opposite angles on the rails using my fingers.

STEP 5 Mark the center of one of the rails. Using a square tooth blade, position the fence so the blade will cut to one side of the centerline. Raise the blade to ½" high and cut a through groove in one edge of all of the rails and stiles. For the stiles, choose either edge for your groove. For the longer top rail, make the groove in the tapered, shorter edge. For the shorter bottom rail make the groove in the wider edge. This can get confusing, so mark the edges to be grooved.

STEP 6 To assure the groove is centered, make the first cut, then turn the rails and stiles 180°, referencing the other side against the fence and make the second cut. This centers the groove in the parts to accept the floating side panel. Make fence adjustments if necessary so the groove is ¼"-wide. After your final pass leave the blade at the same height in order to cut your tenons.

STEP 7 I find it helpful to use a shop-made push block when cutting the tenons. This allows you to clamp the rails to the push block at the appropriate angle. If you don't use a push block or a tenon cutting jig here, the piece could move during a cut—and that can be dangerous. The push block is shown on its side. For the tenons, it is used standing upright with the small block on top.

STEP 8 Cut the tenons by clamping the rail to the push block with the cut end on the rail resting flat on the saw's table. Set the fence so the blade will cut the outer part of the tenon.

93

STEP 9 Turn the rail 180°, making sure the end is flat on the table saw (it will angle the opposite direction), and cut the other side of the tenon. Repeat these two cuts on both ends of all eight rails before moving your fence.

STEP 10 Move the table saw fence slightly toward the blade and make another pass. Turn the rail and make the second pass. Cut both ends of all eight rails at this setting before moving your fence. Continue this process, easing the fence in just slightly, until the tenons fit snugly into the grooves in the stiles. Remember, the distance the fence is moved is double the amount of material being removed. Make small adjustments.

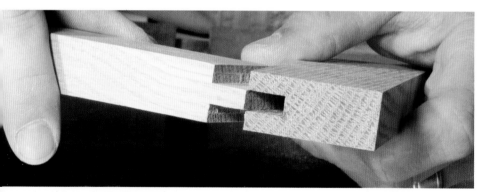

STEP 11 Because you used the same blade height when cutting the grooves for the floating panels and the tenons, the tenons will be the correct length to fit perfectly in the groove. (The grooves for the floating panels also serve as the mortises.)

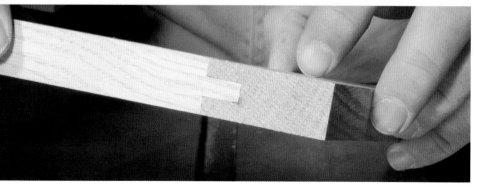

STEP 12 The tops of the stiles will be visable when the wastebasket is finished. Fit the end of the tenons so they bottom out in the grooves. It's not necessary to leave a space for glue.

STEP 13 I chose to resaw and bookmatch the quartersawn white oak to make the floating panels. (This technique requires you to slice a board in half, opening the two pieces like a book. When glued together, one piece is a mirror image of the other.) The graining in the bookmatched panels for this particular piece looks very similar to the stems of a large leaf. You can also make the panel wiht multiple hardwood boards glued together or a piece of ¼"-thick plywood. If you choose to use plywood, find a piece that is veneered on both sides because both sides will be visible.

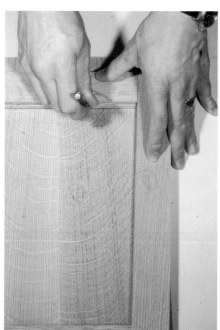

STEP 14 Place a dry-fitted frame on top of each panel and trace a line around the inside of the frame.

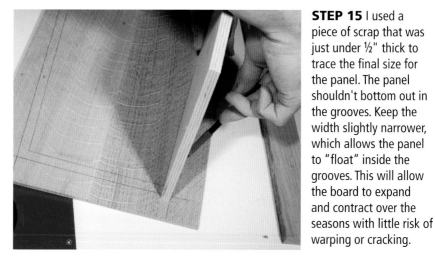

STEP 15 I used a piece of scrap that was just under ½" thick to trace the final size for the panel. The panel shouldn't bottom out in the grooves. Keep the width slightly narrower, which allows the panel to "float" inside the grooves. This will allow the board to expand and contract over the seasons with little risk of warping or cracking.

STEP 16 Cut all the panels to size by cutting on the outside line. It might be helpful to erase or sand off the inside line so you don't cut on the wrong one.

95

STEP 18 If you have access to a jointer, after gluing up the frames, set the jointer fence to 45° and set the infeed table so it takes no more than a ¹⁄₁₆"-deep cut. Make as many passes as necessary to complete the miter (until the face and edge meet at a point). While making the miter, count the number of passes you make on the jointer and cut the remaining miters, making this same number of passes for each one.

STEP 17 If you don't have access to a jointer, it's easier to cut the long miters on the stiles before gluing everything together. Set the table saw blade at 45° and set the fence so the blade will take only enough stock to allow the edge to come to a point. These edges are fragile, so pad the edges during glue up and use very little clamping pressure to avoid damaging the edges.

STEP 19 Set the table saw blade angle at 4° and cut the dado to accept the bottom. It is important to cut the long miters before cutting th is dado. Otherwise, the jointer could cause the small piece of wood at the bottom of the dado to splinter off.

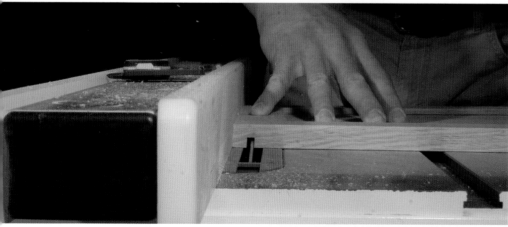

STEP 20 Move the saw's fence and cut the dado to final width.

STEP 21 Using the same 4° blade angle, cut the bevel on the top edge of the frame assemblies. This bevel will allow the completed wastebasket to sit flat on the floor. When cutting the top angle, the inside of the panel faces up (for a left-tilting saw) or down (for a right tilting saw).

STEP 22 Reset the fence to cut the bevel for the bottom edge. The top and bottom bevel cuts should be parallel to each other.

STEP 24 Use a brush to spread glue on all of the miters. To keep the bottom from moving and rattling, put a dab of glue in the center of two opposite bottom dadoes.

STEP 23 Dry fit the frames together and measure for the bottom. After cutting the bottom to fit, lay all four frames on a flat surface with the outsides facing up. Butt the sharp edges of the miters together and tape the three joints.

STEP 25 Insert the bottom, fold the parts together and tape the final joint. I chose to use an oil stain on this wastebasket. Use scrap to try different colors until you come up with one you like. I created my color by mixing five parts red mahogany and one part dark walnut oil-based stains. I applied three coats of wipe-on polyurethane since this piece will be treated like "trash."

Four Ways To Build A Tavern Table

Build almost any table you please with
these tried-and-true construction methods.

by Troy Sexton

We used to have a table just like this one that was great for playing cards or board games with our two kids. Unfortunately, I sold that table and have always regretted it. So after we finished a couple of new basement rooms for the kids, building a new game table was first on my list.

The top of this table is made from three boards of wormy chestnut, a species of wood that you're going to have to hunt for. I bought mine from a wholesaler who bought it out of a barn in the Smokies. And it was expensive: about $10 a board foot. The painted base is made from poplar.

Begin the project by milling the legs and cutting the taper. You can use a tapering jig for your table saw, but I don't recommend it. A few years ago I came up with a quick way to use a jointer to cut tapers faster and safer. See the sidebar "If You Have a Jointer, Throw Your Tapering Jig Away."

There are a lot of ways you can join the aprons to the legs, from totally traditional to quick-and-dirty. I prefer using a straight mortise-and-tenon joint, though if I were building a little side table or something else that wouldn't see daily abuse, the two less traditional methods I'm going to cover would work just fine. But before we talk about the bases, build the top.

The plugs for the breadboard ends are made from the same material as the tabletop. Sand the plug to fit, put some glue on the sides and tap it in place.

I usually build my tables using straight mortise-and-tenon joinery. However, there are special cases when other methods are just as good or even better.

These tabletop fasteners are cheap ($1.99 for a pack of eight) and sturdy. Simply place the clip end into the kerf in your apron and screw the other end to your tabletop.

Making the Top

After I pulled the right boards from my woodpile, I got them ready for glue-up. I wanted this top to look rustic, so I didn't plane the lumber. Instead, I jointed the edges of the planks and glued up the top. Then I rough sanded it with a belt sander to get it reasonably flat and to remove some of the milling marks. Then I cut the top to size and worked on the breadboard ends.

For a long time I used traditional through-mortises to attach breadboards to cover the end grain of my tabletops. Other people showed me how to do it with slotted screw holes. I was always against using that method until I actually tried it. Now it's the only way I'll attach breadboards. You actually get less up-and-down movement using screws, and the top stays flatter-looking for a longer time. Here's how I make my breadboard ends.

After cutting the breadboards to size, cut ⅜"-wide by 2½"-long by 1½"-deep mortises in the breadboards. I cut five of these for my 36"-wide top. However many you use, it's always good practice to use an odd number of mortises so it's easier to lay them out.

I put the two outside mortises ½" in from the end of the breadboard.

Now cut two slots for two screws in each mortise. I make the slots about ⅜" long to give the top some real room to move if it has to. You can make a router jig to cut the slots, or you can use your drill press and work the bit back and forth. Clamp the breadboard to the tabletop and put two screws in each mortise. I put the screws at the sides of the mortise, not at the center. I do this because I peg the fake plug later in the process, and this keeps me from boring a hole into one of my screws accidentally. Don't drive the screws in too tightly because you want the tabletop to be able to move.

Now plug the mortises. I cut plugs to fit the opening and taper them a bit so they fit snugly when tapped in place. Glue the plugs in place, then peg the plugs through the top with ¼" x ¼" square pegs.

Now age the top. I strike the top with a key ring full of keys; I even write people's names in the top with a knife. It's pretty amusing to watch people as they see me do this. They freak out.

Stain the top with a golden oak color and then add a natural oil finish, such as Watco, which is an oil and varnish blend. You don't want the top to look too shiny.

Now turn your attention to the base.

Mortise and Tenon

Cut your aprons to size. Cut 1"-long tenons that are ⅜" thick. The apron lengths in the Schedule of Materials include the tenons. I cut my tenons first and use them to lay out my mortises, which results in less layout, in my opinion. These aprons are set back ¼" from the front of the legs; this is called a setback.

Now cut a bead on the bottom edge of the aprons using a beading bit in your router. Finally, cut a slot on the inside of the aprons for fastening the base to the top. I use metal tabletop fasteners from Rockler (see the Supplies box at left). Rockler sells very sturdy ones, and I recommend them.

Mitered mortise-and-tenon joinery is common on tables with thin legs or when your setback is deeper than normal.

When you have to use mitered mortise-and-tenon joinery, don't get too worked up about the fit of the miter. You don't want the miter too tight.

Some Thoughts on Table Design

No matter which construction method you use to build your table, you must follow a few rules when designing your table. Otherwise your family and guests will be uncomfortable: They'll ram into each other, or they'll constantly bang their knees on your aprons.

We've combed several books on the topic of tables, and most sources agree on these guidelines.

TABLE HEIGHT

You don't have a lot of room to wiggle here. Make sure your table height falls between $28\frac{1}{2}$" and 30". A few sources state that 32" is OK, but 30" or less is more common.

APRON HEIGHT

Make sure each of your sitters has at least 24" to 25" of room between the bottom of the apron and the floor. This means that a 30"-high table with a $\frac{7}{8}$"-thick top should have aprons no wider than $5\frac{1}{8}$".

OVERHANG

The distance from the edge of the top to the apron can vary. Between 10" and 18" is great — if possible.

ELBOW ROOM

The amount of tabletop allowed for each place setting should be no less than 23". A roomier table will have 28" to 30".

TABLETOP WIDTH

The standard width is between 30" and 34". A square table for four should be about 40" x 40". Six can be accommodated by a 60" x 30" top.

CIRCULAR TOPS

To seat four, make your top 44" in diameter ($34\frac{1}{2}$" per person). To seat six people, make it 54" in diameter ($28\frac{1}{4}$" per person).

LEG TAPER

Tapered legs are a common feature of dining tables. Legs should taper down to half their width at the floor. The taper should begin about 1" below the apron.

SOURCES

For more about standard furniture sizes and basic furniture construction, check out the following books:

Rodale's Illustrated Cabinetmaking: How to Construct and Design Furniture That Works by Bill Hylton, Rodale Press, Emmaus, Pennsylvania.

Measure Twice, Cut Once by Jim Tolpin, Popular Woodworking Books, Cincinnati, Ohio.

Encyclopedia of Furniture Making by Ernest Joyce, Sterling Publishing Co. Inc., New York.

Cabinetmaking and Millwork by John L. Feirer, Bennett Publishing Co., Peoria, Illinois.

Be sure to glue the joint and hold the leg and apron together tightly while screwing it together.

Pocket screws aren't my first choice for building dining tables, but for a small occasional table, it'll work.

SCHEDULE OF MATERIALS:
FOUR WAYS TO BUILD A TAVERN TABLE

No.	Item	Dimensions T W L	Material
4	Legs	$2^{1}/_{8}$" x $2^{1}/_{8}$" x $28^{1}/_{4}$"	S
2	Aprons*	$^{3}/_{4}$" x $4^{1}/_{4}$" x $31^{3}/_{4}$"	S
2	Aprons*	$^{3}/_{4}$" x $4^{1}/_{4}$" x $25^{3}/_{4}$"	S
1	Top	$1^{1}/_{8}$" x 36" x 43"	P
2	Breadboards	$1^{1}/_{8}$" x $2^{1}/_{2}$" x 36"	P

P = Primary wood: chestnut

S = Secondary wood: poplar

* = Including 1" tenon

For these fasteners, the slot needs to be the width of your table saw's blade (between $^{1}/_{8}$" and $^{1}/_{16}$" wide) and $^{7}/_{16}$" down from the top of the apron and $^{3}/_{8}$" deep.

Glue up your base, peg the mortises through the legs and finish the base. I use square pegs in my legs. Drill a round hole through the leg and into the mortise. Then take a piece of square stock, whittle one end of it roundish, then pound it into the hole. It should convert your round hole into a square.

Mitered Mortise and Tenon

This method is similar to the straight mortise and tenon above, but you must miter the ends of the tenons because your mortises meet in the middle of the leg. Why would they meet? Well, you might have a thinner leg, or your mortises might be back farther if you chose to use a larger setback.

When this is the case, I make a standard tenon

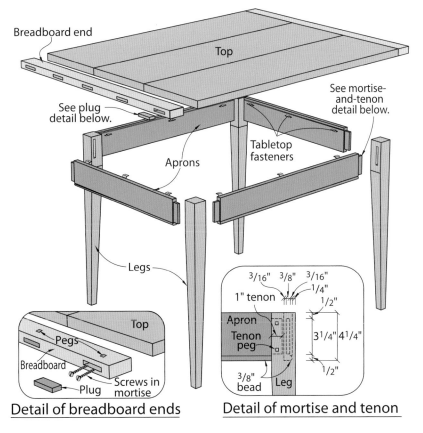

Detail of breadboard ends

Detail of mortise and tenon

and chop the end off at a 45° angle on my miter saw. You're not trying to match the two miters exactly (it will never show), so leave a little gap between the two tenons. If it's too tight, it could get you in trouble because the ends of the tenons will touch before the shoulders seat into the legs.

If You Have a Jointer, Throw Your Tapering Jig Away

For years I used a tapering jig on my table saw to cut tapers on legs. Even after cutting hundreds of the things, I never liked using the jig. It felt unsafe and always brought my fingers too close to the blade for comfort. One day this method came to me out of the blue. It works so well and so fast that I'm still kicking myself for not thinking of it sooner. It uses your jointer and can cut just about any taper in only two quick passes.

Let me show you how to do this on a $2\frac{1}{8}$" x $2\frac{1}{8}$" x $28\frac{1}{4}$" leg. First mark on the leg where the apron will be. Let's say the apron is 4" wide. Add 1" to that and make a mark 5" down from the top of the leg. Then take the remainder of the leg, $23\frac{1}{4}$", divide that number in half and forget about the fraction — so you get 11". Make a mark on the leg that's 11" up from the bottom of the leg. To reduce the width of the leg at the floor by half (which is standard with leg tapering), set your jointer to make a $\frac{1}{2}$"-deep cut. Now make your first pass on the jointer by slowly pushing the leg into the cutterhead — foot first — until you reach the mark at 11". Lift the leg off the jointer.

Now turn the leg around so the top part is headed toward the cutterhead. Place your pusher-hold-down block on the bottom of the leg and push down so you "pop a wheelie" with your leg. Slowly push the leg into the cutterhead while pushing down and forward on your pusher-hold-down block. When you finish this pass you will have a perfectly tapered leg on one side.

Here I am making the first pass on the leg. My jointer is set to make a $\frac{1}{2}$"-deep cut. As soon as the cutterhead reaches the mark at 11", pull the leg up off the jointer.

Here I'm beginning the second pass on the jointer. I've turned the leg around and "popped a wheelie" using my pusher-hold-down block. Advance slowly and steadily into the cutterhead.

Here I am near the end of the second pass. The outfeed table supports the tapered side after it comes off the cutterhead so the leg moves steadily over the jointer beds as long as I keep firm pressure down on the pusher-hold-down block.

Pocket Screws

I wouldn't recommend this for a large table. If you're going to spend the money on the wood, you might as well do it right. But if you want to build a quick-and-dirty side table, this will work fine. Be sure to glue and screw this joint for added strength. It's important to keep the pieces tightly together as you screw the apron to the leg.

Corner Brackets

Corner brackets are a faster alternative to traditional joinery, but they aren't as sturdy. However, you can't beat them when you want to make a table that can be knocked down and stored away.

These measurements apply to the brackets from Rockler (see the Supplies box on page 98). The first step to installing these brackets is to cut a bevel on the inside corner of the legs. This is where you'll later

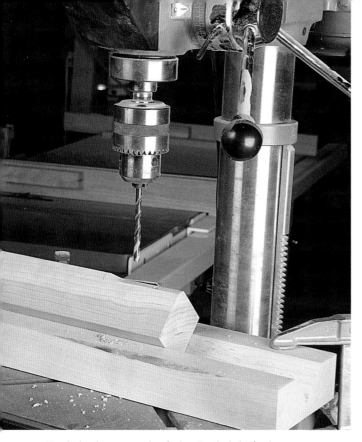

Use the bracket as a template for locating the holes for the corner bracket. Then use a drill press to make your pilot holes.

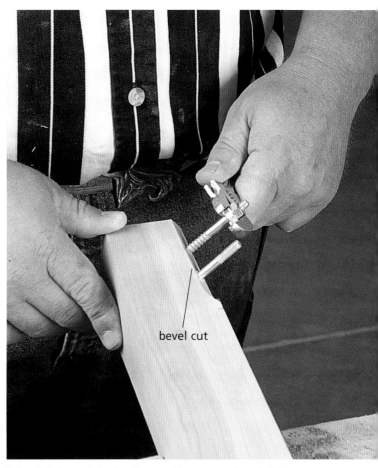

bevel cut

To install the hanger bolts, thread two machine nuts onto the end of the hanger bolt and tighten them against one another. Then grip the two nuts with a wrench and screw the hanger bolts into the leg.

install the hanger bolts. The best way to cut the bevel is on your jointer. Set the machine's fence to a 45° angle and the depth of cut to ¼". Cut 3½" in on the top corner as shown in the photo.

Now install the hanger bolts, which are odd-looking fasteners that have wood screw threads on one end and machine screw threads on the other. The wood screw end goes into the leg, and the machine screw end is bolted to the corner bracket. To install the hanger bolts, first lay out and drill pilot holes on the leg. Then install the bolts using the method shown in the photo.

Now you need to cut a kerf in each apron for the bracket to grab. The kerf should be 1¾" in from the end and ⅜" deep for these brackets. Different brands can use different measurements.

Attaching the Top and Finishing

I attach the top with tabletop fasteners that I screw in place about every foot. On the long aprons, don't push the fasteners all the way into the kerf when screwing them down. This will give your top some room to move.

I finish the base with a couple coats of latex paint followed by a glazing stain. Finally, I add a couple coats of lacquer for protection.

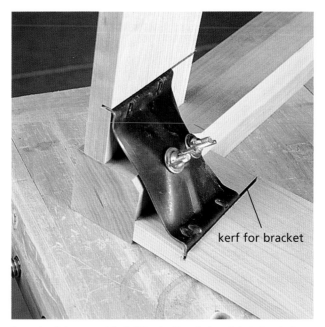

kerf for bracket

Corner brackets are great for building furniture that needs to be knocked down or moved frequently.

Curly Maple Country Wall Shelf

A table saw, router and a few basic
hand tools are all you'll need.

by Steve Shanesy

There are many reasons for the current popularity of country furniture. It not only reminds us of simpler times, but its casual elegance helps produce a friendly, informal setting where we can relax and retreat from the hustle and bustle of our busy, modern world. But these country-inspired styles hold additional appeal for the woodworker, especially those of us with limited time and machines, because like their original antique cousins, country pieces are relatively simple to build with basic tools.

Country woodworkers of the colonial era might have been itinerant tradesmen moving from town to town. Because they were working for clients with less money, the country woodworker combined simple joinery and a modest assortment of tools to build plain furniture for his clientele. Although I used a table saw and router in constructing this wall-hung shelf, it's not difficult to imagine doing all the work with a hand crosscut and rip saw, a chisel or two, and a couple of basic hand planes.

With a nod to the past, I included an element or two that puts this project in the antique reproduction category. I used cut nails, and not only did I dovetail the top rail and drawers, but I used a bevel-edge drawer bottom as well.

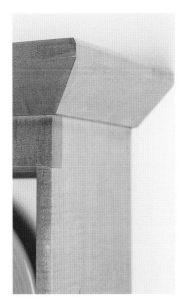

Here's the assembled dovetail on the top rail joining the case side. The top edge, hidden by the crown, was not dovetailed, but simply nailed to the side.

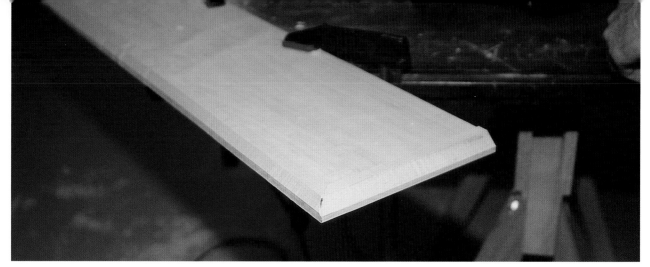
Before assembly, the plain maple bottom is edged with curly maple then chamfered using a router.

Prepare the Stock

Although it's expensive, I selected curly maple, because little wood is required for the project. Cherry or even poplar would also be good choices. Because figured woods such as curly, fiddleback or tiger maple are expensive, I mixed in regular maple in the places where the wood really wouldn't be seen. I also used a less expensive secondary wood for my drawer sides, back and bottom.

Before starting in the shop, I made up my cutting list. I always begin with an accurate, detailed cut list, which was especially helpful in laying out the cutting of the three curly maple boards from which I had to get all my pieces. I was able to plan where the best figure would be showcased in the project and make sure grain direction was balanced and pleasing to the eye.

Because the maple I bought was already surfaced to ¾", the only rough preparation required was to straighten the edges on the jointer. I then cut all my pieces to width and length according to my cutting list. I did, however, put off cutting the crown molding miters and drawer fronts until the case was assembled. As with all projects, cut similar parts on the same setups to maintain consistency and accuracy. Just remember that you'll have rights and lefts, ups and downs, as you proceed through your cutting.
Mill the Joints

Before leaving the table saw, I cut my ¾" x ½"-deep rabbets on the top ends of the two side pieces and on the long edges of the top piece using a dado set. I then made my ¾" x ¼"-deep dado cuts in the sides (to hold the two shelves), and on the bottom side of the lower shelf (to house the two verticals that form the partitions between the three drawers).

Before assembly, I routed a "plate groove" on each shelf top surface, and hand-cut the dovetails and pins for the top front rail where it joins the sides (the back

Country Wall Shelf

	NO.	LET.	ITEM	DIMENSIONS (INCHES)			MATERIAL	COMMENTS
				T	W	L		
❑	2	A	Sides	¾	7	34	P	Rabbet top edge, dado for shelves
❑	1	B	Top	¾	7	32½	P	Rabbet two long edges
❑	1	C	Bottom	¾	7	32½	S	
❑	1	D	Bottom edge	¾	1	51	P	
❑	2	E	Shelves	¾	7	32	P	Run plate groove before assembly, dado bottom shelf for drawer partitions
❑	1	F	Front rail	¾	3	33	P	Half dovetail to sides
❑	1	G	Back rail	¾	3	31½	P	
❑	2	H	Partitions	¾	5½	7	P	
❑	2	J	Plate rails	¾	¾	31½	P	
❑	3	K	Drw. fronts	¾	5¼	10	P	
❑	6	L	Drw. sides	½	5¼	6⅛	S	
❑	3	M	Drw. backs	½	4¹¹⁄₁₆	10	S	
❑	3	N	Drw. bottoms	½	6	9⅜	S	
❑	2	P	Side crn. mld.	¾	3	9	P	
❑	1	Q	Frnt. crn. mld.	¾	3	36¾	P	
❑	3	R	Wood pulls	1" dia.				
❑	6	S	Stop blocks	½	½			

P = Primary (figured maple, cherry or poplar); S = Secondary

rail butts to the sides and is nailed in place). Because the front rail extends to the top rabbet, only the bottom half of the dovetail required cutting.

Part of my stinginess with the curly maple included making the bottom from regular maple, which I edged with 1"-wide x ¾"-thick curly maple. An added benefit was that no end grain showed on the bottom, and the curly grain is especially striking with the bevel detail on the sides and front. When gluing the edges, a spline or biscuit is required for the end grain of the bottom but unnecessary for joining the long grain to long grain on the front edge. It's important to rout the bevel detail before assembly.

Assemble the Case

Unless you want to hold parts in place while assembling, clamps are not required, because all joints are nailed using the antique-looking square cut nails. In fact, you could make a case for eliminating glue as well, but gluing is an old habit of mine that's just too hard to break.

First assemble the lower shelf and drawer partitions. Because these are nailed from the top down, it's easier to swing a hammer now rather than when it's assembled with the sides and upper shelf. The cut nails are anything but delicate, and with their wedged shape, are prime candidates for causing splits. I overcame this potential hazard by drilling a pilot hole for each nail. It's also important to consider a nice spacing arrangement for the nails, rather than just accepting arbitrary, approximate locations. (Just because you're using nails doesn't mean it's not furniture!)

The sides, shelves and top came next. Each was set in its dado or rabbet and nailed. I then attached

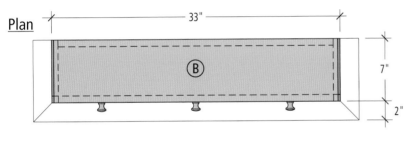

Plan

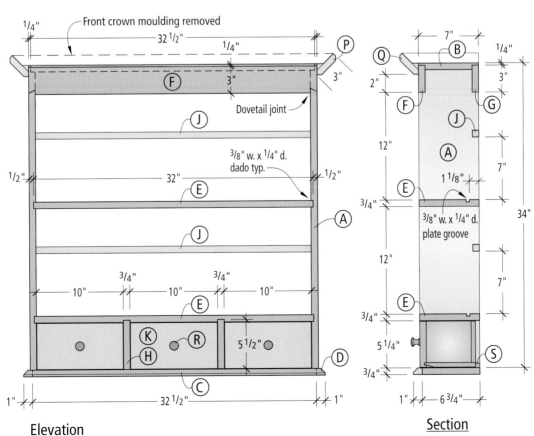

Elevation

Section

Illustration by John Hutchinson

109

the front top rail in its dovetail and nailed it where it sits in the rabbet of the top. I likewise nailed the back rail in its rabbet, and also nailed it through the side. With this complete, I was then able to turn the piece upside down to set the bottom in place and nail it. I used two nails each for the sides and drawer partitions. Again, I drilled pilot holes for each nail.

Make and Attach the Crown

Everything having to do with the crown moulding was

Crown profile

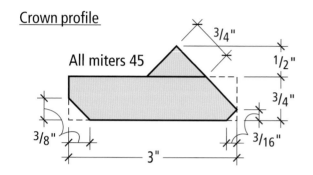

The crown compound miter is cut on the table saw. Tilt the blade to 30° and the miter gauge to 35°.

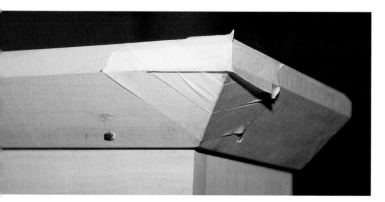

A simple method for "clamping" the crown when gluing is using masking tape – just pull it tight over the joint.

110

done on the table saw. Its shape was made by simply making two 45° angle cuts, one for the bottom and one for the top. Before cutting, however, I laid out the profile of the crown and quickly concluded that an extra triangular shaped piece would be needed on the backside to create a sufficient flat to nail it easily to the case. This was accomplished simply enough by cutting an equilateral triangle with ¾" legs. The triangular-shaped piece was glued (not nailed) in place so that it lined up with the angle cut on the bottom edge.

After cutting the angles on the long edges of the board (giving the crown its final profile), I cut the compound miters where the sides of the crown meet their corresponding front. This was accomplished easily enough on the table saw by setting the blade to a 30° angle and the slot miter gauge to 35° (see the picture below). With careful measurements and thoroughly thinking through the cuts (I had to be careful; I was working with the last piece of curly maple in the shop!), the crown parts were complete. To attach the crown to the case, I nailed the parts on with the bottom of the crown 1" down from the top of the case. To pull the compound miter joint together, I used a few pieces of masking tape (as shown at left). This technique was much faster and simpler than cutting clamping cauls to just the right shape, which would be an absolute requirement if one were to use clamps to do the job.

Cut and Assemble the Drawer Parts

All three drawers are the same size. The curly maple fronts were cut from the same board and kept in sequence so that the grain matched across. The sizes provided in the cutting list are for ½" sides, backs and bottoms with a ¾" front. I used half-blind dovetails for joining the sides to the front and back. If you use a different construction method, your sizes will change, except for the drawer openings.

I used a Porter-Cable dovetail jig outfitted with a template for making ½" dovetails and box joints. Although these, and most other jigs, take some precise setup, they produce nice, repeatable results. For this project, I would have preferred Porter-Cable's template that makes 2" dovetails because these would have given a more "hand cut" look. But as is, I'm satisfied with the look achieved using the ½" template. The drawer bottoms were made in the traditional style of a bevel-edged panel. The bevel is cut in the same manner as raised panels on the table saw. Simply tilt the blade to about 15° and run the panels on edge. Calculate the fence setting so that the bevel you make fits nicely into a ¼" x ¼" groove that starts ¼" from the bottom edge of the drawer sides and front. Using half-blind dovetails required me to make a stopped dado for the drawer bottom groove in the drawer front. To mill the dado, I used a router set up on the router table with a ¼" straight bit. I trimmed the back so that its width is ½" narrower than the sides, which allows the bottom to slip in from behind. The drawers are small enough to slip simply in and out of their openings with no guide system required. For pulls, I purchased turned round knobs at the local hardware store.

Finishing

Because the parts were pre-sanded to 120 grit before assembly, I picked up the sanding chore using 150 grit with the random-orbit palm sander. I proceeded to 220 grit and finished sanding by breaking all the sharp edges with 120-grit sandpaper.

Because I wanted the shelf to look as if it was already a number of years old, I mixed brown and yellow aniline dye stain to give it a honey color, the approximate color a shellac finish on maple might attain after years of exposure to light. To avoid the splotchiness of maple and stain, I sprayed the aniline dye stain and immediately wiped it down with lacquer thinner on a clean rag. This evened the color for good consistency.

I topped the color with a water-based lacquer that I sprayed on. After the first coat dried after 45 minutes, I sanded it with 360-grit paper, then sprayed a second wet coat. It dried to a smooth finish. To create a little contrast, I sprayed the pulls black using black lacquer from an aerosol can and then topped them with a coat of clear lacquer.

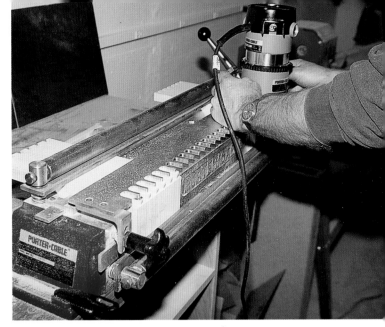

Drawer sides were joined to the front and back using ½" half-blind dovetails cut on a dovetail jig.

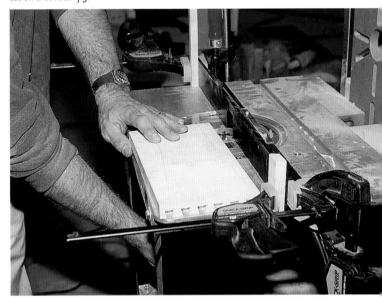

A stopped groove was required on the inside of the drawer front to receive the bottom. It was cut with a router.

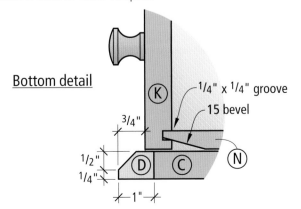

Bottom detail

K
¼" x ¼" groove
15 bevel
3/4"
½"
¼"
D   C   N
1"

The drawer bottoms are ½" thick but are beveled to slip into a ¼" groove, a traditional drawer construction method.

Stepstool

by Thane Lorbach

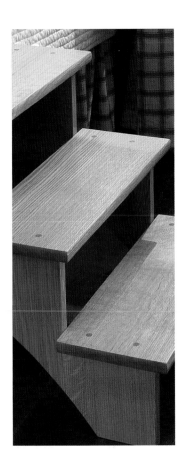

A stepstool is a necessity in every home. Most aren't very attractive. Until I built this design, mine was always hidden in a closet. At my house, this piece functions as both a stepstool and a place for my kids to sit. It is, in fact, a piece of furniture. You can build this project in a weekend or less and it's not difficult to do. If you want to build a piece of furniture but need to hone your woodworking skills, this is a great project to take on.

The construction is straightforward, and you can complete the entire piece using basic tools. Buy your wood already surfaced (flat and square) and the main power tools you will need are a table saw, jigsaw or band saw, and a drill. In the course of this project you will make matching risers, learn a fun way to draw a curve and use dowels to hide screws and lend a decorative look to your work. So, step right up...

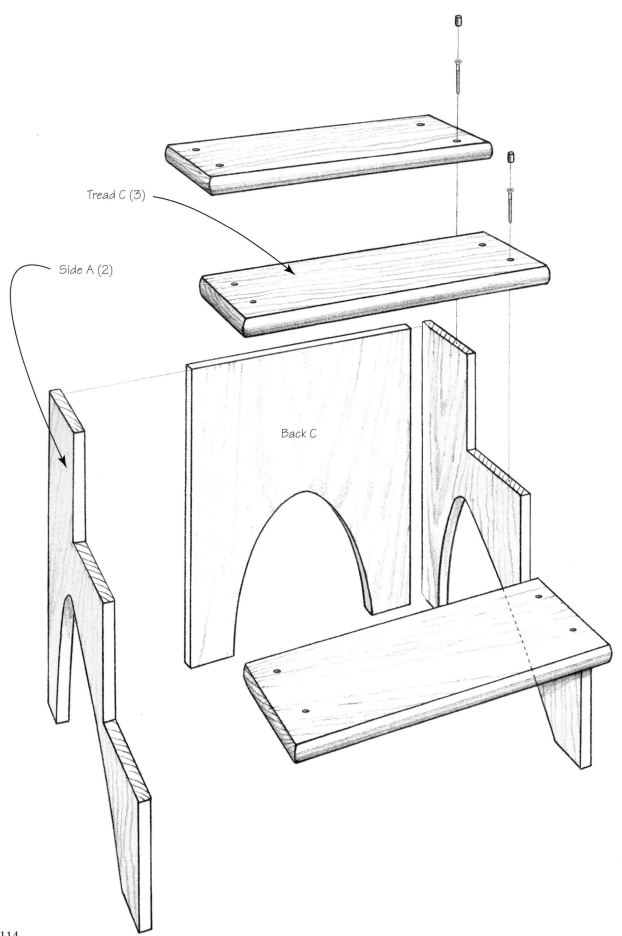

Tread C (3)

Side A (2)

Back C

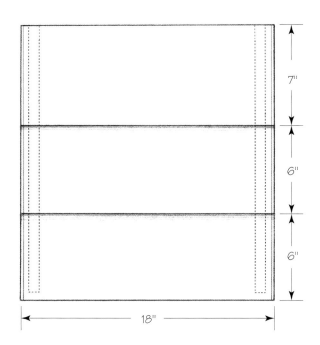

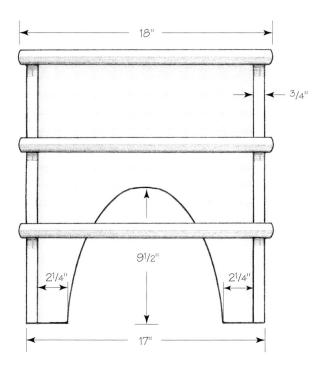

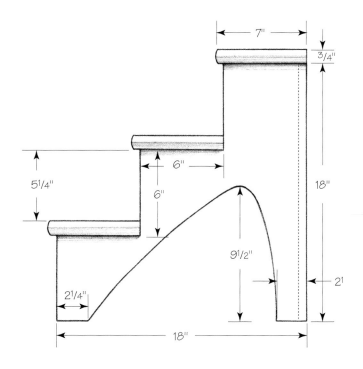

INCHES (MILLIMETERS)

REFERENCE	QUANTITY	PART	STOCK	THICKNESS	(mm)	WIDTH	(mm)	LENGTH	(mm)
A	1	sides	white oak	3/4	(19)	18	(457)	18	(457)
B	1	back	white oak	3/4	(19)	15 1/2	(394)	18	(457)
C	2	threads	white oak	3/4	(19)	7	(178)	18	(457)

HARDWARE & SUPPLIES

- 24—No. 8 × 2" (50mm) flathead wood screws
- wood glue
- stain
- polyurethane finish

STEP 1 After purchasing or milling all of the stock, rip all parts to width. To make the back, edge glue as many pieces of wood as needed to achieve the final width.

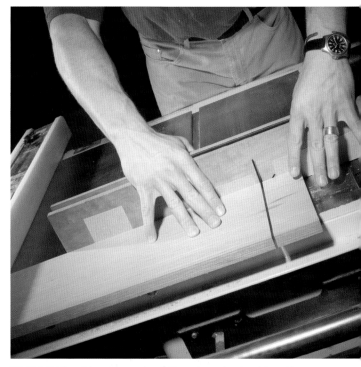

STEP 3 The sides are made of three boards glued together to create the notches for the steps. Reference the squared end of the side boards against the fence. Cut the two longest side boards and the back boards to length. Move the saw fence and cut the middle side boards. Set the fence again and cut the shortest side pieces.

STEP 2 Square up one end of each board and mark that end using a pencil.

STEP 4 I found it easiest to glue up the sides two boards at a time using a spacer cut to step height.

STEP 5 Glue the short sideboard in place to complete the side assembly. (The bottom board square, so make sure the grain runs vertically.)

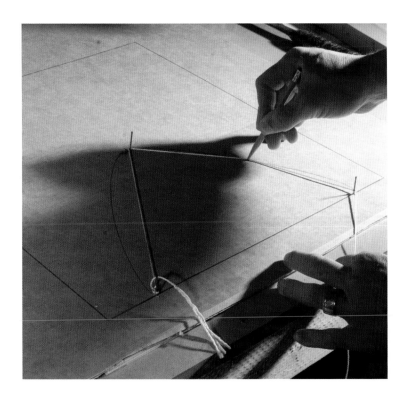

STEP 6 To visually lighten the stepstool and to add some personal creativity to the project, I cut curves in the back and both sides. After gluing the boards together to make the back, lay the back on a piece of cardboard a couple inches from the bottom edge and draw a line around the perimeter. Determine how tall and wide you want your curve to be. Place a sacrificial board (plywood or medium density fiberboard [MDF]) under the cardboard and drive a nail at the curve's tallest point in the center (left to right) of the back. Drive nails on the bottom line at the curve's widest point, one on each side. Tie a string onto the bottom left nail, bring it over the top nail and loop it twice around the bottom right nail. Place a pencil inside the string and draw the curve. Loosen or tighten the string to form the curve you want. The looser you have the string, the wider and rounder your curve will be. For the curves in the sides, follow the same procedure, but offset the top nail instead of centering it. Once you have your desired curves drawn on cardboard, cut them out with a utility knife and use them to draw the curves onto the back and sides of your project. Using a jigsaw or band saw, cut out the curves in both sides and the back. Then use a file and sandpaper, or a spindle sander, to clean up the saw marks.

STEP 7 Lay the sides back edge to back edge. Mark the screw hole locations for attaching the sides to the back.

STEP 8 Because the back is ¾" thick, drill the holes ⅜" from the back edge of each side using a countersink bit. Drill the holes so the countersink bit creates a ¼"-deep hole that will accept a plug to hide the screw head.

STEP 9 Sand the inside of the back. Then clamp the back and sides together and install the screws. You can use glue in addition to screws but it's not necessary.

STEP 10 Using part of a roundover router bit, ease the front edges and ends of the treads. Rout the end-grain first, taking a very light pass. Routing the long-grain after routing both ends cleans up any tear-out caused by routing the end-grain. Mark the back edges of the treads so you don't accidentally roundover the back edges. A file, rasp, sandpaper or block plane can also be used to create the roundover on the treads.

STEP 11 After sanding the entire piece (sides, back and treads), attach the treads to the base assembly using screws and wood plugs. Cut a scrap piece of wood the same width as the back and place it between the two sides at the bottom step so the sides will remain parallel. Start with the bottom tread. For a more dramatic look, choose a contrasting wood for the plugs.

My kitchen has a white oak floor with a natural finish so I chose not to stain this piece. Since this piece will get a lot of wear, I applied four coats of polyurethane, rubbing with No.0000 steel wool between each coat — including the final coat — for a nice semigloss look.

Applying stain and polyurethane can change the wood's color and appearance, so use some scrap wood from your project as a test piece. Experiment with different stains and finishes.

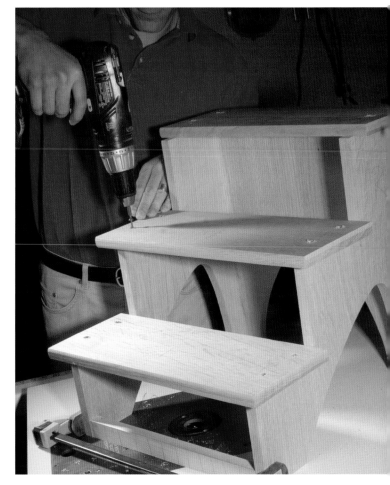

Drop-Leaf Kitchen Table

by Andy McCormick

This elegant little drop-leaf table is perfect for an eat-in kitchen or efficiency apartment. With its leaves raised, it's 48" in diameter, but with both leaves dropped, it narrows to 24" wide.

Installed in the base is a handy double-faced drawer that you can open from either side. Anything from silverware and placemats to hammers and pliers can be stored in the drawer.

The design of this table is simple but with enough style to fit almost anywhere. The base can be painted, as I have done, or it can be made of wood that matches the top and finished natural.

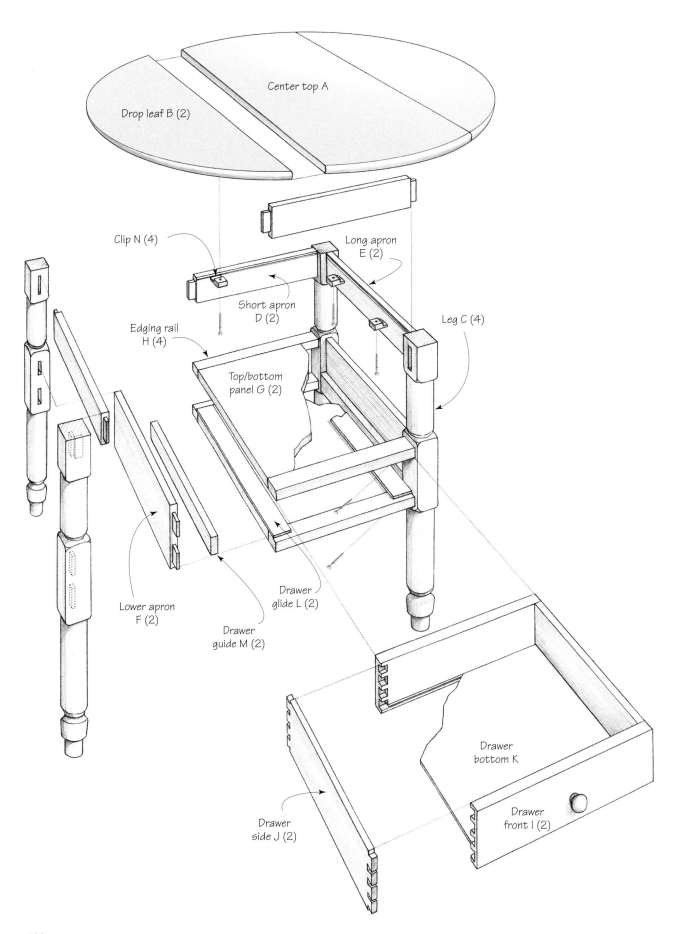

Center top A

Drop leaf B (2)

Clip N (4)

Long apron
E (2)

Short apron
D (2)

Edging rail
H (4)

Leg C (4)

Top/bottom
panel G (2)

Drawer
glide L (2)

Lower apron
F (2)

Drawer
guide M (2)

Drawer
bottom K

Drawer
front I (2)

Drawer
side J (2)

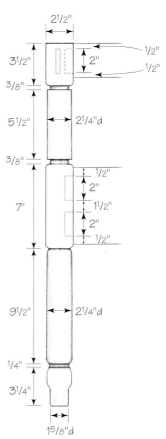

LEG DETAIL

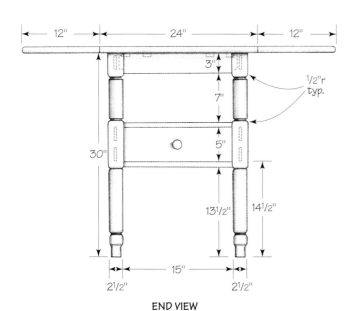

TOP VIEW

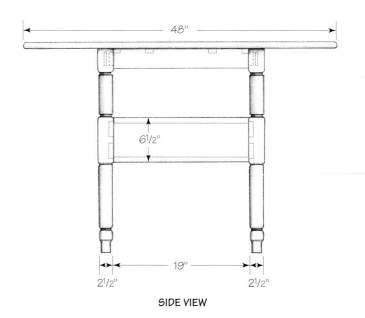

END VIEW

SIDE VIEW

cutting list

REFERENCE	QUANTITY	PART	STOCK	THICKNESS		WIDTH		LENGTH		COMMENTS
A	1	center top	cherry	¾-⅞	(19-22)	24	(610)	48	(1219)	
B	2	drop leaves	cherry	¾-⅞	(19-22)	12	(305)	48	(1219)	
C	4	legs	poplar	2½	(64)	2½	(64)	30	(762)	
D	2	short aprons	poplar	¾	(19)	3	(76)	16½	(419)	length includes ¾"-long tenons on both ends
E	2	long aprons	poplar	¾	(19)	3	(76)	20½	(521)	length includes ¾"-long tenons on both ends
F	2	lower aprons	poplar	¾	(19)	6½	(165)	20½	(521)	length includes ¾"-long double tenons on both ends
G	2	top & bottom panels	birch ply	¾	(19)	16¾	(425)	19	(483)	
H	4	edging rails	poplar	¾	(19)	2	(51)	15	(381)	
I	2	drawer fronts	poplar	¾	(19)	4¾	(121)	14¾	(375)	
J	2	drawer sides	poplar	½	(13)	4¾	(121)	21⅞	(556)	
K	1	drawer bottom	birch ply	¼	(6)	14¼	(362)	22	(559)	
L	2	drawer glides	poplar	⅛	(3)	2	(51)	19	(483)	
M	2	drawer guides	poplar	1	(25)	2	(51)	19	(483)	
N	4	clips	poplar	¾	(19)	1	(25)	2	(51)	

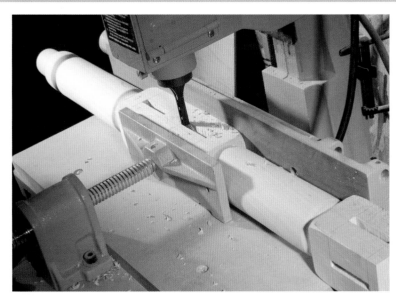

hardware & supplies

- 1 pair—metal drop-leaf supports
- 2 pair—drop-leaf hinges
- No. 20 biscuits
- 4—No. 8 × 1" (25mm) wood screws
- paint for base
- stain
- clear finish

STEP 1 After turning the legs to shape, cut the mortise slots. This can also be done with a router and a jig, a router mounted under a router table or a drill press with a Forstner bit followed by cleanup with a chisel.

STEP 2 Cut the cheeks for the tenons first.

STEP 3 One of the easist ways to cut the tenon faces is to use a tenoning fixture at the table saw. The tenons can also be cut using the same setup shown in step 2. Incrementally move the apron away from the fence and nibble the material away. Do this on both faces.

STEP 4 The band saw is great for cutting the tenon offset. Complete the offset by cutting the scrap away with a hand saw.

STEP 6 Make sure you do the leg assembly glueups on a flat surface so everything stays flat. Also, check for squareness. (If everything has been cut properly, the sides should go together perfectly.)

STEP 7 Using the short aprons, attach the two base side assemblies together.

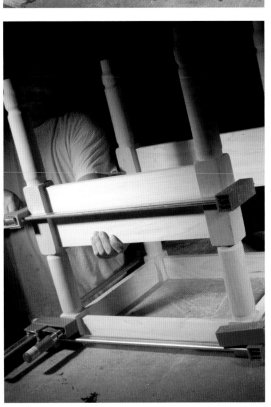

STEP 5 When the mortises and tenons have been cut and dry fitted, assemble the two sides of the base.

STEP 8 Using glue, pocket holes and screws, attach the top of the drawer box.

STEP 9 Using glue and pockets screws, attach two edging rails to each end of the top of the drawer box.

STEP 10 Attach the bottom of the drawer box and two edging rails to the table base using the same method shown in steps 8 and 9.

STEP 11 Attach the drawer guides using glue and nails. Note that the guide is about 1/16" proud of the inside faces of the legs. This will keep the drawer fronts from hitting the legs.

STEP 12 Install the drawer glides with glue. The glides automatically create the proper gap between the bottom of the drawer front and the bottom of the drawer box. These glides also help the drawer glide smoothly.

STEP 13 The drawer sides (left) are dovetailed into the drawer fronts (right). I cut these dovetails using a router jig and a router setup with a dovetail bit. They're not fancy but they are strong and look good when the drawers are assembled.

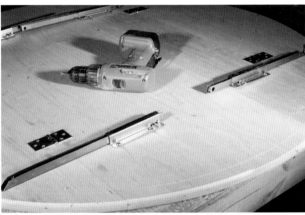

STEP 14 Glue up enough hardwood boards to create the proper widths needed for the center top and the two drop-leaves. Then attach the parts to each other using drop-leaf hinges. Install the drop-leaf supports.

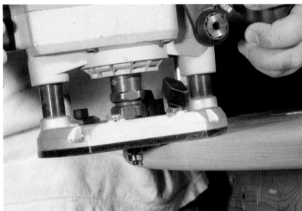

STEP 15 Using a router setup with a roundover bit, cut a roundover on the bottom and top edges of the tabletop. A chamfer instead of a roundover also looks good.

STEP 16 The top is attached to the base using wooden clips that you can make on the table saw. After making sure that all is working properly, remove the top from the base. Now you can paint or stain the base and finish the top. Re-attach the top and you're ready to sit down to a well deserved meal.

Medicine Cabinet

If you've never built a face frame cabinet, learn the tricks that ensure a square-looking case, tight joints and doors that work as you build this small cabinet.

by Troy Sexton

I've built hundreds of single-door cabinets like this one. Some people use them as spice cabinets. Others use them in the bathroom as a medicine cabinet. As I was building this particular cabinet, it occurred to me that it would be an excellent project for beginners. It has all the traditional components of larger-scale cabinetry, yet it doesn't need a lot of material or tooling. Once you've built this cabinet, you can build something bigger using the same principles. Intermediate woodworkers might also pick up a trick or two because I build my cabinets just a bit differently.

Choose Your Wood

I used tiger maple for this project, but if this is your first cabinet, you might want to use poplar and then paint the finished item. Poplar is easy to work with and less expensive than maple, especially if the maple has some figure.

As in larger cabinets, most of the major components are made from ¾"-thick stock: the case sides, top, bottom, plus the rails and stiles for the door and the face frame. This cabinet has a solid-wood shiplapped back that's made from ½"-thick pieces; the door panel is ⅝" thick.

Face Frame: The Place to Start

It seems logical to begin by constructing the case. Don't. The size of your case and door are all determined by your face frame. Build it first and then you'll use your face frame to lay out your case and door. All face frames are made up of rails and stiles, much like a

door. The stiles are the vertical pieces. The rails are the horizontal pieces that go between the stiles.

When you rip your stiles to width on your table saw, make the rip ¹⁄₁₆" wider than stated on the Schedule of Materials. You need this extra to overhang the sides of your case so you can trim it flush with a flush-cutting bit in a router. Once your pieces are cut to size, join the rails and stiles using mortise-and-tenon joints.

Begin by cutting the tenons on the rail ends. I know the books say to cut the mortise first, but I've found it's easier to lay out your mortises after your tenons are cut. Try it, and I think you'll agree.

The tenons should be ⅜" thick (one-half as thick as your stock), centered on the rail and 1" long. I cut ½" shoulders on the tenons. If they're any smaller, the mortise might blow out. Now use your tenons to lay out your mortises on the stiles. Hold the tenon flat against the edge where the mortise will go and use the tenon like a ruler to mark your mortise.

Now cut your mortises. Make them all 1¹⁄₁₆" deep, which will prevent your 1"-long tenons from bottoming out. You don't want your tenons to wobble in your mortises, yet you don't want to have to beat the tenon in place.

Dry fit your face frame, then put glue on the mortise walls and clamp it up. While you're waiting for it to dry, turn your attention to the bead moulding that goes on the inside edge of the face frames.

Years ago, I used to cut the beading into the rails and stiles. Then I would have to miter the bead and cut away the beading where the rails and stiles were joined. It sounds like a pain, and it was. Now I simply make my bead moulding separate from my face frame and miter, nail and glue it in place. It looks just as good.

To make the bead moulding, put a ¼" beading bit in your router and mount it in a router table. Then take a ¾"-thick board that's about 4" wide and cut the bead on one edge. Take that board to your table saw, set your rip fence to make a ⅜"-wide cut and rip the bead from the wide board. Repeat this process three more times.

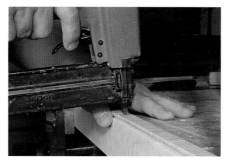

Adding this beaded moulding to the inside of the face frame creates a nice shadow line around the door. Miter, glue and nail it in place. Don't forget to putty your nail holes.

Now take your strips and run them through your planer to reduce them in thickness to 5⁄16". Miter the corners; then glue and nail them in place. Sand both sides of your face frame with 100-grit sandpaper and move on to building the door.

The Door

Why make the door next? Well, for one thing, it is easier to hang your door in your face frame before you nail the face frame to your case.

I build my doors so they are the same size as my opening, then I shave off a little so there's a 1⁄16" gap all around. This way if the door or face frame is out of square, I can taper the door edges to fit, hiding my error.

The door is built much like the face frame, using the same size mortises and tenons. The biggest difference is that you will need to cut a groove in your rails and stiles for the door panel, so your tenons must be haunched. A *haunch* is a little extra width in the tenon's shoulder that fills in the groove on the end of the stile.

Fit your door in the face frame before you attach the face frame to the case. Everything lays flat on your bench as you work. You'll find this procedure is a faster and easier way to get perfect results.

Begin by cutting a ⅜"-deep by ⅜"-wide groove down the center of one long edge of your rails and stiles. Cut your tenons on your rails. Then cut your mortises on your stiles. Dry fit the pieces together and measure how big the center panel should be.

You want the panel to float to allow seasonal expansion and contraction, so cut the panel to allow ⅛" expansion on either side. Now raise the door panel using

your table saw or a cutter in your router table. Practice on scrap pieces of ⅝" stock so you achieve the right lip, angle and fit.

When the panel is complete, sand the raised section, then glue up the door. Be careful not to get any glue in the groove that holds the panel. When the glue is dry, hang the door in your face frame.

Finally, the Case

The case is simple. The top and bottom pieces fit into ¼"-deep dadoes and rabbets on the sides. The back rests in a rabbet on the sides and is nailed to the back edge of the top and bottom pieces.

You'll use your face frame to lay out your joints on the sides. You want the bottom piece to end up 3⁄16" higher than the top edge of the bottom rail on your face frame. This allows your bottom to act as a stop for the door. Mark the location of that ¼"-deep dado and cut. The top piece rests in a ¼"-deep by ¾"-wide rabbet on the sides. Cut that using your table saw. Then cut the ½"-deep by ¼"-wide rabbet on the back edge of the sides.

Drill holes for shelf pins and space them 1" apart on the sides. Sand the inside of the case. You'll notice that the top and bottom are ½" narrower than the sides. This is to give you a good place to nail the back pieces to the case. Assemble the case using glue and nails, making sure the top, bottom and sides are all flush at the front.

Attach the face frame to the case using glue and nails. Trim the face frame flush to the case using a bearing-guided flush-cutting bit in your router. Finish sand the cabinet to 180 grit.

Take your scrap pieces and use them to make a shiplapped back. Cut a ¼" x ½" rabbet on the edges and then cut a bead on one edge using a ¼" beading bit in your router table. You want to give the back pieces room to expand and contract, about ⅛" between each board should be fine.

Cut the moulding for the top so it resembles the drawing detail below. Finish sand everything, then nail the moulding to the top.

I like to peg the tenons in my doors to add a little strength. Drill a ¼"-diameter hole most of the way through the stile and tenon. Then whittle a square piece of stock so it's round on one end, put glue in the hole and pound it in place. Cut the peg nearly flush. You want it to be a little proud of the stile — it's a traditional touch.

Break all the edges of the case with 120-grit sandpaper, and putty all your nail holes. Paint, dye or stain all the components. I used a water-based aniline dye. Then add two coats of clear finish and nail the back pieces in place. Hang the cabinet by screwing through the back boards into a stud in your wall.

cutting list

NET			
No.	Item	Dimensions T W L	
2	Face frame stiles	¾" x 2¼" x 30"	
1	Top face frame rail	¾" x 2⅞" x 15½"	
1	Bottom face frame rail	¾" x 1½" x 15½"	
2	Door stiles	¾" x 2½" x 25"	
1	Top door rail	¾" x 2½" x 9⅞"	
1	Bottom door rail	¾" x 3½" x 9⅞"	
1	Door panel	⅝" x 8⅜" x 19½"	
2	Case sides	¾" x 6" x 30"	
2	Top & Bottom	¾" x 5½" x 17"	
4	Shelves	¾" x 5$\frac{7}{16}$" x 16$\frac{7}{16}$"	
	Back boards*	½" x 17" x 30"	
	Top moulding	¾" x 2" x 36"	

*Use any number of random-width boards to create the back, totalling 17" in width.

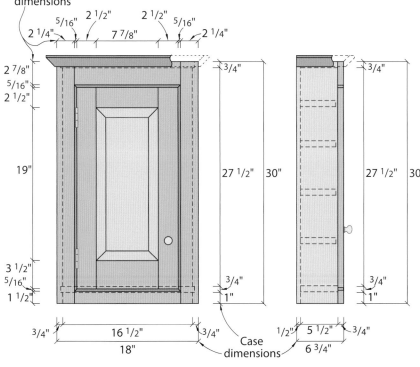

supplies

Rockler, (800) 279-4441
www.rockler.com
• hinges for door, #31495, $8.99/pair

Horton Brasses Inc.
(800) 754-9127
www.horton-brasses.com
• machine screw fitting, #K-12 w/MSF, call for pricing

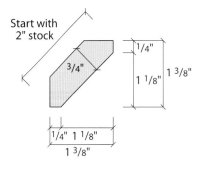

Here you can see how the bottom of the case acts as a door stop. This is one of the reasons I build my face frames first: I can make sure my bottom will be in perfect position.

Fit the face frame on the case. The stiles should hang $\frac{1}{16}$" over the edge of the case so you can rout (or plane) them flush later.

Antiqued Tabletop Hutch

This hutch can be placed on a counter or tabletop, or hung on a wall.

by David Thiel

This hutch could be used in a variety of home settings, but our reason for offering it to you is as a training piece on creating a simple, but stunning, antique finish.

The wood used for this project should have a reasonably tight grain and be fairly inexpensive. In our part of the country, poplar fits the bill. Start by cutting the pieces to the sizes given in the Schedule of Materials.

Using the template provided, mark and cut the shape on the sides, then sand the edges to smooth the profile.

Next, cut a ¼" × ¼" through-rabbet on the back inside edge of each side, and stopped rabbets of the same dimension on the top and bottom. Stop the rabbets 1¼" from each end.

Now rout the edge treatment of your choice on the front and side edges of the top and bottom pieces. I used a simple ogee bit.

Before the hutch can be assembled, notch the two dividers and the center shelf with bridle joints (also called egg-crate joints) to form the six drawer openings. Lay out and mark the location for the shelves on the sides and nail the shelves in place. Next nail the top and bottom to the sides, slide the divider section into place and nail through the shelf and bottom to hold it in place.

Double-check the drawer sizes against the Schedule of Materials, then cut the drawer pieces to size. I used rabbeted joinery to provide a little extra strength to the drawers. Cut a ¼" × ½"-wide rabbet on both inside ends of the fronts, and another ¼" × ½"-wide rabbet on the back ends of each side. Next cut a ¼" × ¼" groove on the inside bottom edge of each drawer side and front, starting the groove ¼" up from the bot-

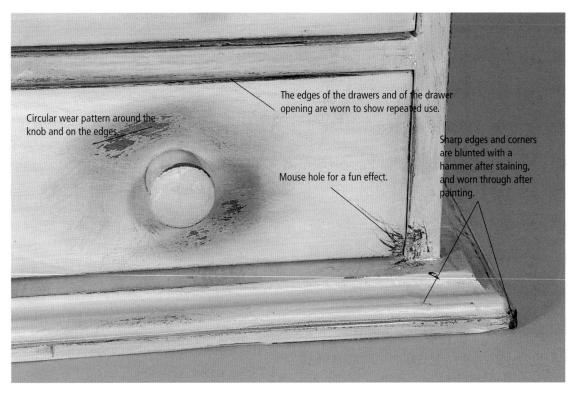

Circular wear pattern around the knob and on the edges.

The edges of the drawers and of the drawer opening are worn to show repeated use.

Mouse hole for a fun effect.

Sharp edges and corners are blunted with a hammer after staining, and worn through after painting.

Shown above are a few results of simple distressing techniques. The stained level of the finish shows through behind the paint, and the paint is worn in areas that would likely see use through the years. The antiquing was done with a gray 3M pad. The mouse hole was done with needle-nose pliers.

tom edge. Assemble with nails, holding the drawer backs flush to the top of the drawer sides to allow the drawer bottoms to slip into the side grooves under the drawer back. Leave the drawer bottoms loose at this time.

Cut the hutch back to size and attach the knobs to the center of each drawer. Now you're ready to put an antique finish on the piece.

The finish is a six-step process. The first is to stain the entire piece as it would have been done originally. While this stain will be covered with paint, you should approach it with almost the same care as if it were your final finish. If your final paint color is light, the underlying stain should be dark to provide strong contrast. I used a brown mahogany gel stain on the piece and stained everything, including the inside of the drawers.

Now have a little fun. Use a ring of keys, a hammer or a screwdriver and beat on the piece a little. The idea is to provide the appearance of decades worth of wear, not abuse. It's tempting to go overboard. Think about how the damage you are inflicting could have happened — corners on the moulding would be dented, edges would be blunted, and the drawers would have seen a fair amount of use. This is only the

middle of the antiquing process, so don't go too far.

The next step is to apply a coat of paint to the piece. This would be a point in the hutch's life when it had fallen out of favor and had been relegated to the pantry or cellar. Because of this, the paint job wouldn't be too neat or perfect, but rather an effort to cover the damage to the original stain.

With the paint dry, get the keys back out and add some more "time" to the piece. As a next antiquing step, take some steel wool or an abrasive pad and wear through the paint at points of high contact. This would be around the knobs, where the drawers slide against the top and bottom surfaces of the cabinet, the edges of the shelves and on the edges of the sides.

With the paint finish distressed, add a coat of brown glaze to the piece, immediately wiping most it off after applying. The remaining glaze will leave a discolored look to the paint, and highlight the new dings and scrapes.

As a final step, add a coat of flat or satin clear finish to protect the paint and glaze.

Your completed antique hutch can be placed on a counter or tabletop or can be hung on a wall. Enjoy it, and happy antiquing!

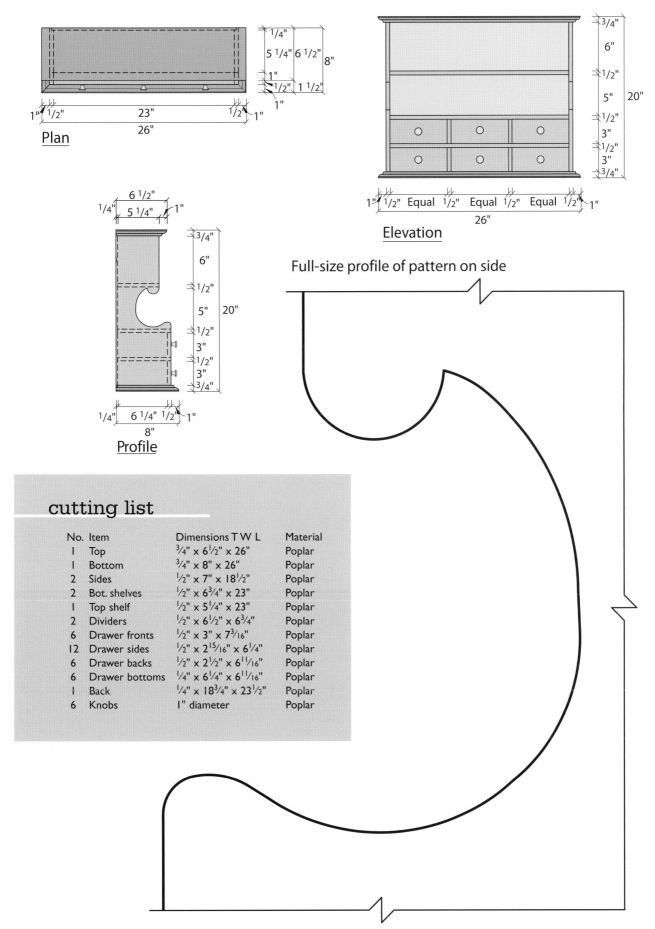

Plan

1/4" 5 1/4" 6 1/2" 8"
1"
1/2" 1 1/2"
1"
1" 1/2" 23" 1/2" 1"
26"

Elevation

3/4"
6"
1/2"
5" 20"
1/2"
3"
1/2"
3"
3/4"

1" 1/2" Equal 1/2" Equal 1/2" Equal 1/2" 1"
26"

Profile

6 1/2"
1/4" 5 1/4" 1"
3/4"
6"
1/2"
5" 20"
1/2"
3"
1/2"
3"
3/4"
1/4" 6 1/4" 1/2" 1"
8"

Full-size profile of pattern on side

cutting list

No.	Item	Dimensions T W L	Material
1	Top	3/4" × 6 1/2" × 26"	Poplar
1	Bottom	3/4" × 8" × 26"	Poplar
2	Sides	1/2" × 7" × 18 1/2"	Poplar
2	Bot. shelves	1/2" × 6 3/4" × 23"	Poplar
1	Top shelf	1/2" × 5 1/4" × 23"	Poplar
2	Dividers	1/2" × 6 1/2" × 6 3/4"	Poplar
6	Drawer fronts	1/2" × 3" × 7 3/16"	Poplar
12	Drawer sides	1/2" × 2 15/16" × 6 1/4"	Poplar
6	Drawer backs	1/2" × 2 1/2" × 6 11/16"	Poplar
6	Drawer bottoms	1/4" × 6 1/4" × 6 11/16"	Poplar
1	Back	1/4" × 18 3/4" × 23 1/2"	Poplar
6	Knobs	1" diameter	Poplar

Lamp Table

by Bill Hylton

Though it has no specific antecedent, this round occasional table displays common country motifs: simple tapered legs, scroll-cut aprons and a painted finish. Its size and height makes it adaptable for a variety of uses.

The tapered legs are slightly splayed to increase the table's stability, but their feet don't reach beyond the perimeter of the tabletop. The aprons, whose ends are cut at a slight angle, produce the splay. The shelf is captured in notches sawed into the legs.

The router figures prominently in the table's construction. The mortises are cut with a plunge router, and both the tabletop and shelf are cut with a router and trammel. The aprons' scrollwork is refined with a router and template.

Built a couple of centuries ago, this country table would have been painted from bottom to top. In the ensuing decades, daily use would have worn the paint off the top's surface and the edges of the shelf. Rather than mimic the wear of time, the stand is painted and the white oak top has a durable varnish finish.

The tabletop is made of white oak, a widely available domestic hardwood. It's attractive and durable and, because the stock is quarter-sawn rather than flat-sawn, it moves less in width and is likely to hold its roundness through the seasons. The stand is built of poplar, a low-cost, widely available hardwood that works easily and takes paint well.

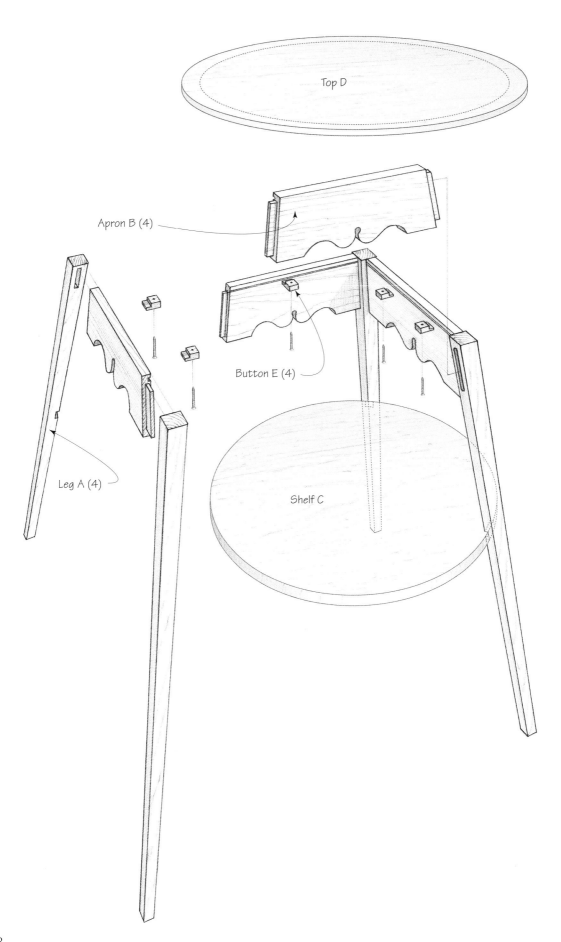

Top D

Apron B (4)

Button E (4)

Leg A (4)

Shelf C

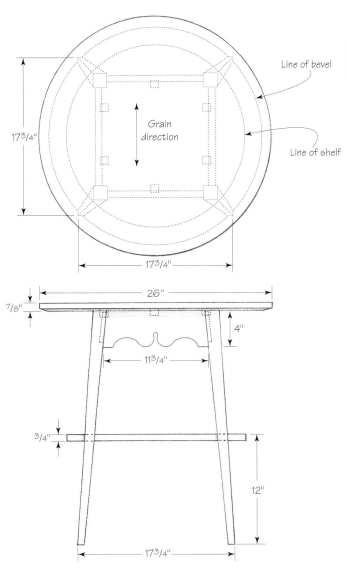

17³/₄"

Grain direction

Line of bevel

Line of shelf

17³/₄"

26"

7/8"

4"

11³/₄"

3/4"

12"

17³/₄"

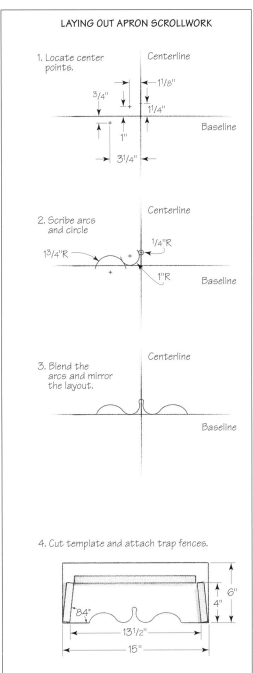

LAYING OUT APRON SCROLLWORK

1. Locate center points.

Centerline

1¹/₈"

3/4"

1¹/₄"

1"

3¹/₄"

Baseline

2. Scribe arcs and circle

Centerline

1¹/₄"R

1³/₄"R

1"R

Baseline

3. Blend the arcs and mirror the layout.

Centerline

Baseline

4. Cut template and attach trap fences.

6"

4"

84°

13¹/₂"

15"

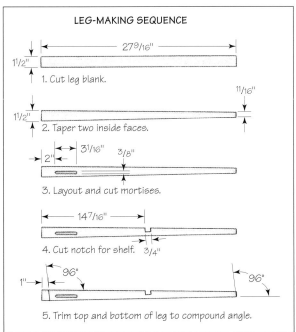

LEG-MAKING SEQUENCE

27⁹/₁₆"

1¹/₂"

1. Cut leg blank.

1¹/₂"

11/16"

2. Taper two inside faces.

2"

3¹/₁₆"

3/8"

3. Layout and cut mortises.

14⁷/₁₆"

4. Cut notch for shelf.   3/4"

1"

96°

96°

5. Trim top and bottom of leg to compound angle.

cutting list

REFERENCE	QUANTITY	PART	STOCK	THICKNESS		WIDTH		LENGTH		COMMENTS
A	4	legs	poplar	1½	(38)	1½	(38)	27½	(699)	will be cut to 26½" (673mm) during construction
B	4	aprons	poplar	⅞	(22)	4¼	(108)	13½	(343)	width be cut to 3⅞" (98mm) during construction
C	1	shelf	poplar	¾	(19)	24	(610)	24	(610)	final diameter of shelf determined during construction
D	1	top	white oak	13/16	(21)	28	(711)	28	(711)	cut 26" (660mm) dia. top from glued-up panel
E	6	buttons	poplar	¾	(19)	⅞	(22)	1¼	(32)	

hardware & supplies

- 6—No. 6 × 1¼" (30mm) wood screws
- paint for table base
- clear finish for tabletop

STEP 1 Crosscut 12/4 stock to about 2" longer than the leg length specified on the cutting list. Face joint and plane the stock the minimum needed to create flat parallel faces. Joint an edge and rip the stock into four oversize blanks. Cut a 1⅝" square window in a piece of cardboard and use this template to lay out a leg on the end grain of each oversize blank. Orient the layout so the annular rings (marked by the red line in the photo) run diagonally.

STEP 2 Rip the individual legs from the oversize blanks with the blade tilted to match the angle of the layout. Since the layout orientation on each blank is likely to be different, you'll have to adjust the tilt (and the fence position) for each blank. Place the blank behind the blade and tilt the blade until it aligns with the layout. Then set the fence so the cut will align with the layout.

STEP 3 Make the bevel cut, creating a base surface so the three remaining rips can all be made with the blade square to the saw's table. Since the degree of blade-tilt needed for this cut will likely vary from blank to blank, you'll need to set up for each cut individually. Make this cut on each blank before making the squaring cuts.

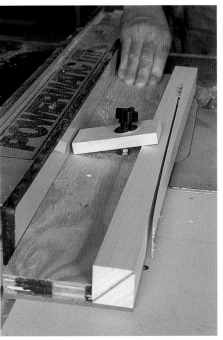

STEP 4 Reset the blade square to the table and make a second cut on each blank. You'll have to reposition the rip fence to align this cut against the individual layouts. After making a second cut on each blank, set the fence at 1⅝" (41mm) and make all the remaining cuts.

STEP 5 Taper the legs. There are several ways to do this. I suggest doing it with a simple fixture (shown at left) on the table saw. Once you've made the jig, sawing the tapers is a matter of two rip cuts per leg. Set the first leg in the jig and secure it with the clamp. Set the rip fence to accommodate the narrow end of the jig with the leg. Feed the jig and leg along the fence. Because the jig holds the leg at an angle to the blade, you'll rip a taper. Loosen the clamp and rotate the leg 90° to the right (so the just cut face is up). Repeat the cut, tapering the adjacent face. In the same way, make two cuts on each of the remaining three legs. As you taper the legs, save the wedges of waste; you'll use them when you glue up the stand.

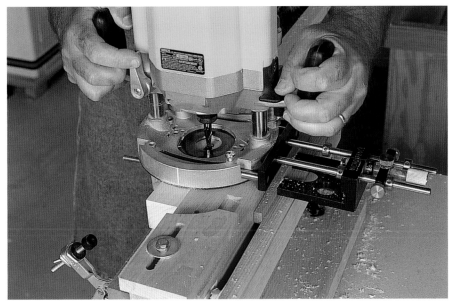

STEP 6 Cut the mortises. You can do this job with a hollow-chisel mortiser, but I used a plunge router, edge guide and a shopmade jig. The fixture holds the leg and supports the router. The router's plunge controls the final depth and the edge guide positions the cut. Stops on the fixture limit the length of the cut. Because of the leg's taper, the mortises are slighter deeper at the upper end than the lower one, and that's OK.

STEP 7 Lay out a mortise on one leg, as shown in the photo; use this sample to set up the fixture and router. Mark the other mortise locations only with the registration line, which corresponds to the middle of the cut. Once the equipment is set up, all mortises will be identical as long as you clamp the leg in the fixture with the untapered faces against the workrest and the fixture back, with the line on the leg aligned with the fixture's registration line. The leg extends left for some mortises and right for others.

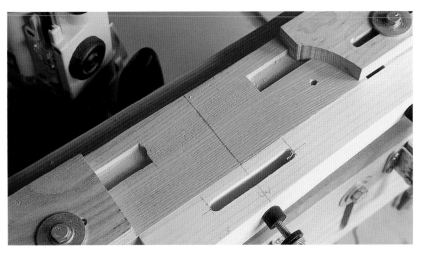

STEP 8 Notch each leg for the round shelf using dado cutter. Set it up to perfectly match the thickness of the shelf stock and tilt to 6°. Cradle the leg in a V-block so the cut is in the arris of the leg and guide the leg across the cutter with the miter gauge. When you set up, position the V-block so it grazes the cutter. Clamp it to the miter gauge.

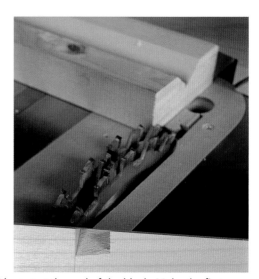

STEP9 Set the mark you made on the leg during your original layout at the end of the block. Make the first cut in the first leg with the cutter deliberately set low. Measure the result and raise the cutter so the resulting cut is ⅜"-deep. Cut each leg.

STEP 10 Trim leg tops to the layout marks. The cut is a compound angle with a 6° bevel and a 6° miter.

STEP 11 Prepare the stock for the aprons. Joint and plane it to the specified thickness, rip it to width and crosscut four pieces slightly longer than the finished size. Reduce them to the desired length as you miter the ends. Here, a pair of aprons are being mitered at one time.

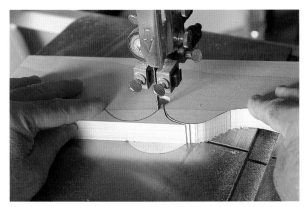

STEP 13 Use the template as a pattern to mark the contour on each apron (trace along the template edge with a pencil). Take the four aprons to the drill press and bore the center hole in each one with the ½" (13mm) Forstner bit. Take them to the band saw next and saw just outside the traced line on each, roughing out the contour.

STEP 12 Lay out the apron contour on a piece of hardboard, following the drawing "Laying Out Apron Scrollwork" on page 137. Begin with a piece that's 8" × 15". Lay out the full contour, then cut it out. Drill the center hole first with a ½" Forstner bit. With a jigsaw, saw as close to the line as possible. Smooth the contour with coarse sandpaper or a half-round file.

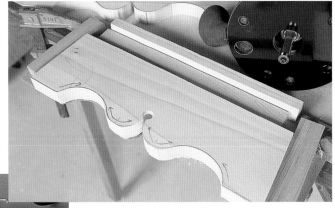

STEP 14 Set up the template by clamping it so the guiding edge overhangs the workbench. Install a flush-trimming bit in your router and adjust the bit extension so the pilot bearing on the tip rides along the template when the router is resting on top of the workpiece. Before you rout any of the aprons, look at the arrows penciled on the apron in the photo. Given the rotation of the bit, you risk splitting a chunk off the convex shape if you move the router "uphill" across the grain. To prevent this, always move the router so the bit is cutting "downhill" across the grain. Follow the arrows, in other words. Yes, you'll be climb cutting portions of the contour, but you shouldn't have any trouble controlling the router.

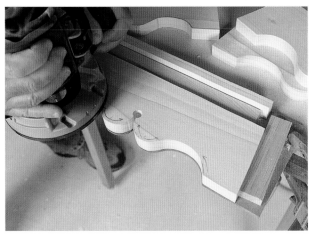

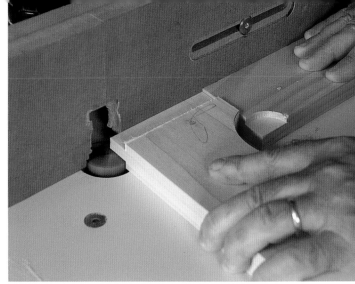

STEP 15 Set an apron on the template. The fences force the workpiece into the right position and prevent it from moving. The router holds it down as you cut. Rest the tool on the work with the bit clear of the edge. Switch it on and trim the work's edge flush with the template edge. Be mindful of the appropriate direction to move the router. Because of the narrow passage at the center of the control, you won't be able to address the entire contour. Use a file to smooth the edges you can't get to with the router bit.

STEP 16 Form the cheeks of the tenons on the router table. The best bit to use is a large-diameter mortising bit (intended for routing recesses for hinge leaves) or a bottom-cleaning bit. A large-diameter straight bit will work too. As you creep up on the optimum depth of cut, make test-cuts on scraps of the apron stock and fit the resulting tenons to a mortise in one of the legs. Set the fence of the router-table produce the correct tenon length. To cut a tenon cheek, butt the apron end against the fence and slide it along the fence and across the bit. You can cut the full depth in a single pass.

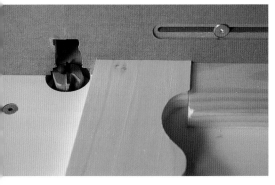

STEP 17 Use a scrap as a pusher to back up the stock edge and prevent tear-out. Because the aprons are mitered at a 6° angle, you must miter the end of the pusher as well. Orient the pusher so its end is in full contact with the edge of the workpiece. When you turn the apron over, you also must turn over the pusher.

STEP 18 The mortise-and-tenon joint has a deep shoulder at the top. The cleanest way to cut this shoulder is on the table saw. Elevate the blade 1" and tilt it 6°. Attach a facing to the miter gauge that's taller than the apron width. Kerf the facing and extend a line from the kerf to the top of the facing. Stand the apron on its top edge and align the tenon shoulder at the line (inset). Kerf the tenon. Turn the apron around, align the shoulder with the line and kerf the second tenon. Cut these shoulders on all four aprons.

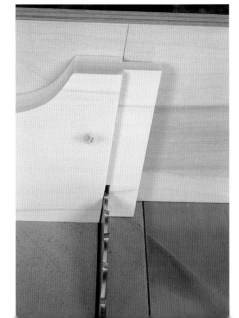

STEP 19 With a square, lay out the edge cuts—one at the top and one at the bottom. The cuts should be perpendicular to the tenon shoulder. Make the cuts on the band saw.

STEP 21 The final step is to chamfer the inside corner of each tenon. The mortises in each leg intersect. To allow the tenons to penetrate the mortises fully, you have to trim them slightly. The task can be done with a chisel or block plane. I chucked a chamfer bit in the router table to do the job uniformly.

STEP 20 The ends of the mortises are rounded, so round off the tenon corners with a pattern-maker's rasp. Be careful not to nick the tenon shoulders with the rasp.

STEP 22 Glue up two legs and one apron. Use the wedges you made when you tapered the legs as clamping cauls. Apply a pipe clamp across the outside of the assembly, along the top edge of the apron. Turn the assembly over and apply a second clamp along the bottom edge of the apron. Assemble the other two legs to an apron in the same way.

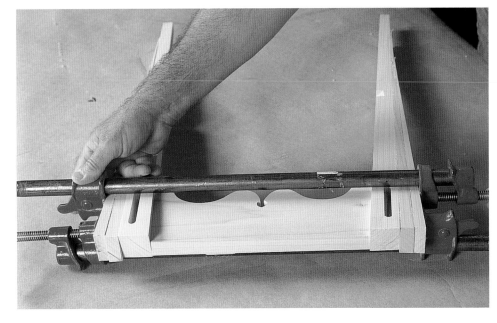

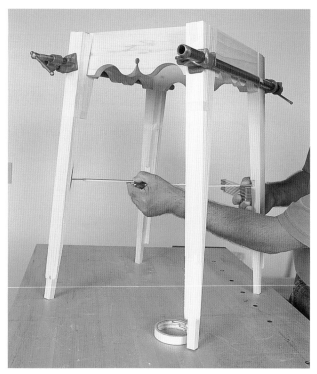

STEP 23 After the glue sets, dry assemble the two subassemblies with the remaining two aprons. (Use masking tape to attach the cauls to the legs, so you don't need an extra pair of hands to apply the clamps.) With a yardstick or folding rule, measure diagonally from shelf-notch to shelf-notch. The distance is the diameter of shelf you need.

STEP 24 With a router and trammel, cut the shelf to the desired diameter. Set the shelf blank, bottom-side up, on an expendable piece of plywood or hardboard and clamp it at two corners to the workbench. Locate the pivot and drill a shallow hole for the pivot screw. Set the router's plunge depth to no more than $\frac{1}{16}$" more than the shelf thickness. Adjust the trammel for the radius of the cut (the bit should be outside the radius). Attach the trammel at the pivot point and cut the shelf. You'll need four to six passes to cut through the stock without overtaxing your router and bit.

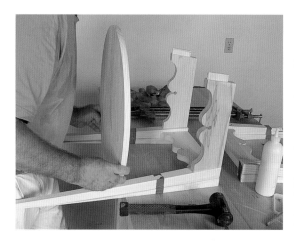

STEP 25 After the shelf is sanded and ready for final assembly, make a practice run. Don't open the glue until you have the cauls taped to the legs, the clamp jaws set and you know—because you've tried it—that everything fits together.

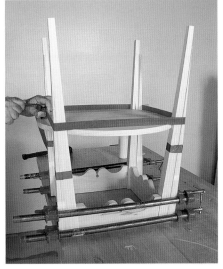

STEP 26 Lay a leg-and-apron subassembly on the bench. Apply glue to the mortises and tenons and fit the two remaining aprons to the subassembly. Apply glue to the shelf notches. Set the shelf into the notches. Apply glue to the mortises in the second leg-and-apron subassembly, to its shelf notches and to the exposed tenons of the aprons. Set the second subassembly in place using a dead-blow mallet to seat it. Tip the assembly upside down and apply pipe clamps. Then drop a band clamp over the legs and tighten it to pull the legs tight against the shelf.

STEP 27 Cut the table with the router and trammel, the same way you did the shelf. The only differences are the size and the stock.

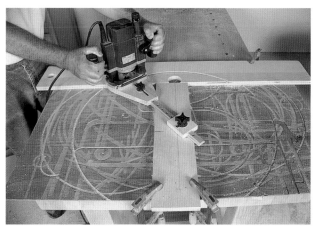

STEP 28 Make a curved fence to use for beveling the underside of the tabletop. Cut the bevel with a horizontal panel-raising bit, which should be used only in a router table. Because you want only the bevel and not the tongue, you can't guide the cut with the bit's pilot bearing, hence the fence. Though the radius of the fence's curve is the same as the tabletop's, the bit must be inside the radius, so the trammel's pivot must be readjusted. Clamp the fence across the bench on top of the sacrificial plywood. Locate the pivot for the arc you need to cut, clamp a scrap there and attach the trammel pivot to it. Rout the arc.

STEP 29 Bevel the underside of the tabletop. Install a straight-bevel panel raiser in your router table. Clamp the fence to the table. (You'll need to bore a clearance hole in the fence for the pilot bearing.) Make sure the fence is positioned to eliminate the tongue-forming portion of the bit; you want only the bevel. A hold-down to help you keep the work tight to the table is useful, but the setup doesn't accommodate the featherboards. The hold-down I used looks odd but works great. To cut, turn on the router with the work clear of the bit. When the bit is up to speed, push the tabletop against the work and move it counterclockwise. A chalk mark can serve as a benchmark, so you know when you've turned the work a full 360°. It's a good idea to stage the cut, starting with a shallow cut and achieving the full depth on the third pass.

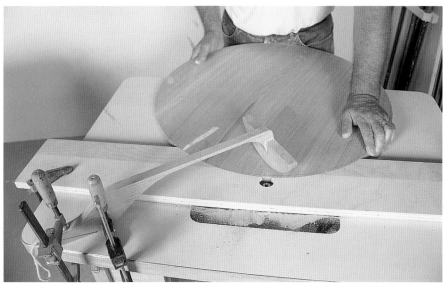

STEP 31 Make the buttons. Select a wide piece of ³⁄₄"-thick stock and cut a ¹⁄₂" wide by ⁹⁄₁₆" deep rabbet across each end. Cut a strip 1¹⁄₄" long from each end of the board, then cut the strip into ⁷⁄₈"-wide buttons. Drill a pilot hole through the center of each.

SREP 30 Cut grooves in the aprons for the mounting buttons. You do this now because the aprons are canted, and it is simply easier to groove them after the stand is already assembled. Attach your router to a long plywood strip that will span the stand. (You can mount it temporarily with carpet tape.) Use a ¹⁄₄" slot cutter. Adjust the cutter so the top edge of the groove is ⁵⁄₈" from the top edge of the stand. Cut a single slot into two aprons and two slots into each of the others.

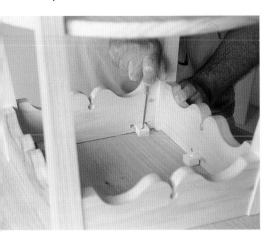

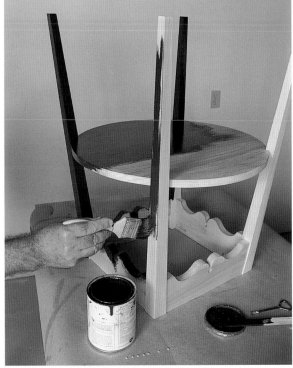

STEP 32 Mount the tabletop before applying a finish. Set the tabletop, top surface down, on the bench top. Upend the stand and line it up on the tabletop. Fit a button into each slot you cut. Use an awl to locate pilot holes for buttons. Remove the stand, and drill the pilot holes.

STEP 33 I finished the top and the stand separately. The tabletop received several coats of rub-on finish. Between coats, I buffed with No.0000 steel wool. I rubbed out the final coat with paste wax and steel wool. I primed the stand with dewaxed shellac, then applied two coats of oil-base paint.

Corner Wall Cabinet

by Kerry Pierce

The design antecedents of this little corner cupboard are difficult to identify. The corner cabinet form has a long history in the genre of American country furniture and some of the details — the band sawn profile at the bottom of the cabinet, for example, suggest early antecedents. However, the mouldings were cut with late 19th-century planes and the scallops below the doors were borrowed from a late 19th-century source. So, although it is clearly a piece that has historical roots, those roots reach out in several directions.

No matter what its history, I like the way it looks.

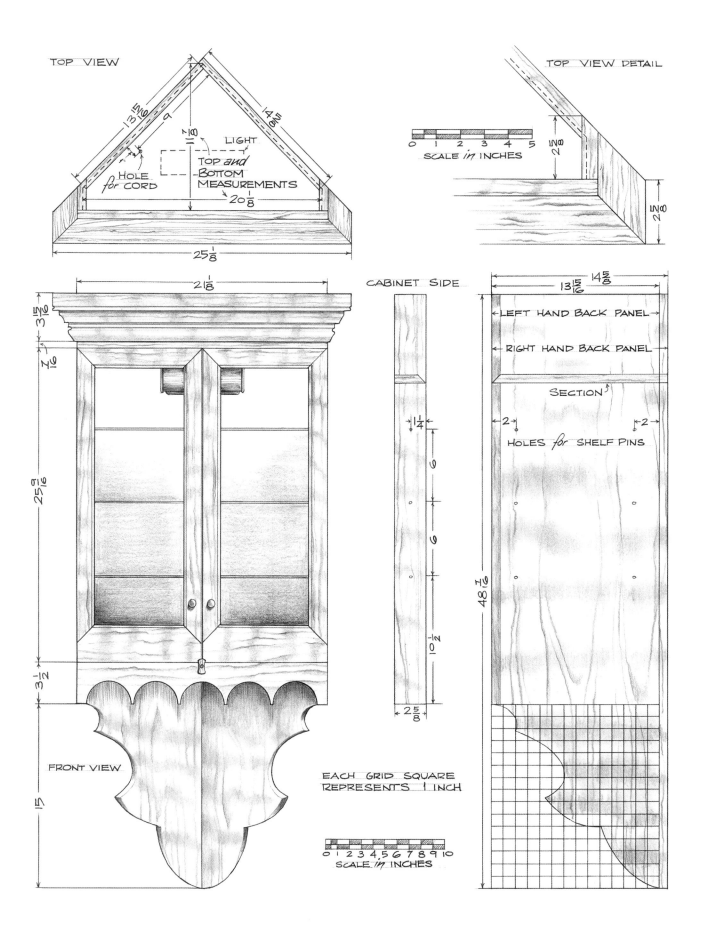

TOP VIEW

TOP VIEW DETAIL

13 15/16   9   14 5/8

1 7/8

HOLE for CORD

LIGHT

Top and Bottom MEASUREMENTS

20 1/8

25 1/8

SCALE in INCHES
0 1 2 3 4 5

2 5/8

2 5/8

21 1/8

CABINET SIDE

13 15/16   14 5/8

3 5/16

7/16

LEFT HAND BACK PANEL

RIGHT HAND BACK PANEL

SECTION

2   2

HOLES for SHELF PINS

25 9/16

1 1/4

6

6

10 1/2

2 5/8

48 7/16

3 1/2

FRONT VIEW

EACH GRID SQUARE REPRESENTS 1 INCH

15

SCALE in INCHES
0 1 2 3 4 5 6 7 8 9 10

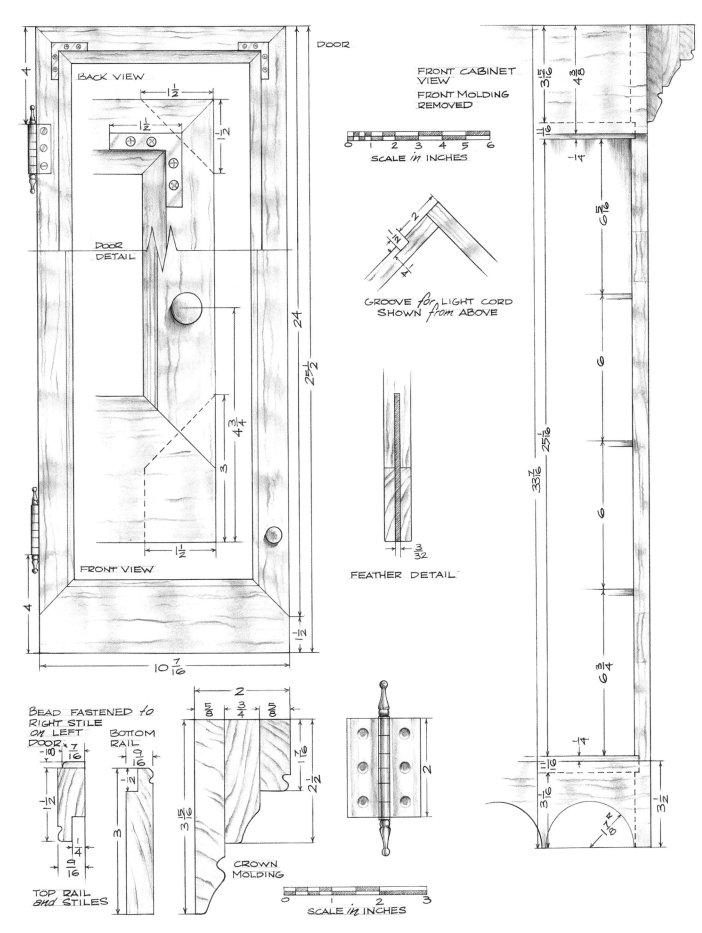

DOOR

BACK VIEW

DOOR
DETAIL

FRONT VIEW

$1\frac{1}{2}$

$1\frac{1}{2}$

$1\frac{1}{2}$

$4\frac{3}{4}$

3

$1\frac{1}{2}$

4

4

24

$25\frac{1}{2}$

$1\frac{1}{2}$

$10\frac{7}{16}$

FRONT CABINET
VIEW

FRONT MOLDING
REMOVED

SCALE *in* INCHES
0 1 2 3 4 5 6

GROOVE *for* LIGHT CORD
SHOWN *from* ABOVE

2

$\frac{1}{2}$

$\frac{1}{4}$

FEATHER DETAIL

$\frac{3}{32}$

$3\frac{15}{16}$

$4\frac{3}{8}$

$\frac{11}{16}$

$\frac{1}{4}$

$6\frac{5}{16}$

6

6

$6\frac{3}{4}$

$\frac{1}{4}$

$1\frac{1}{16}$

$3\frac{1}{16}$

R $1\frac{1}{8}$

$3\frac{1}{2}$

$33\frac{7}{16}$

$25\frac{1}{16}$

BEAD FASTENED *to*
RIGHT STILE
on LEFT
DOOR

$\frac{7}{16}$
$\frac{7}{10?}$

$1\frac{1}{2}$

$\frac{1}{4}$

$\frac{9}{16}$

TOP RAIL
and STILES

BOTTOM
RAIL

$\frac{9}{16}$

$1\frac{1}{2}$

3

2

$\frac{5}{8}$ $\frac{3}{4}$ $\frac{5}{8}$

$\frac{7}{16}$

$2\frac{1}{2}$

$3\frac{15}{16}$

CROWN
MOLDING

2

SCALE *in* INCHES
0 1 2 3

153

cutting list

REFERENCE	QUANTITY	PART	STOCK	THICKNESS		WIDTH		LENGTH		COMMENTS
A	1	right back panel	maple	11/16	(17)	14 5/8	(371)	48 7/16	(1230)	
B	1	left back panel	maple	11/16	(17)	13 15/16	(354)	48 7/16	(1230)	
C	1	right cabinet side	maple	11/16	(17)	2 5/8	(67)	33 7/16	(849)	
D	1	left cabinet side	maple	11/16	(17)	2 5/8	(67)	33 7/16	(849)	
E	2	top and bottom	maple	11/16	(17)	11 7/8	(302)	20 1/8	(511)	
F	1	filler strip under crown	maple	11/16	(17)	4 3/8	(111)	21 1/8	(536)	
G	1	face below doors	maple	11/16	(17)	3 1/2	(89)	21 1/8	(536)	
H	1	top crown moulding	maple	5/8	(16)	3 1/8	(79)	40	(102)	
J	1	mid. crown moulding	maple	3/4	(19)	4 3/8	(111)	40	(102)	
K	1	bott. crown moulding	maple	5/8	(16)	3 15/16	(100)	40	(102)	after gluing moulding parts together, cut to needed lengths
L	4	door stiles	maple	9/16	(14)	1 1/2	(38)	24	(610)	
M	2	door top rails	maple	9/16	(14)	1 1/2	(38)	10 7/16	(265)	
N	2	door bottom rails	maple	9/16	(14)	3	(76)	10 7/16	(265)	
P	8	splines	maple	1	(25)	7	(178)	32 3/8	(822)	
Q	2	arm supports	maple	3/32	(2)	1 1/2	(38)	1 1/2	(38)	cut to fit

hardware & supplies

- 20—No. 8 × 1 5/8" (40mm) drywall or carcase screws
- 12—No. 8 × 2" (50mm) drywall or carcase screws
- 2—5/8" (16mm) × 5" (130mm) lag bolts
- 3—tempered glass shelves 1/2" (6mm) × 1 15/16" (287mm) × 19 1/2" (495mm)
- 4—brass decorator hinges Woodcraft No.16R47
- 1 bag—brass bracket-style shelf supports Woodcraft No. 27114
- 2—brass knobs
- 1—curio cabinet light

STEP 1 Glue up the panels for the cabinet's two back sections, making sure they remain flat under clamping pressure.

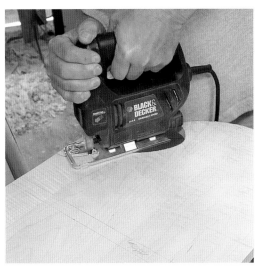

STEP 2 After panels have been planed to flatness, rip them to width (be sure the outside edge of each panel is ripped at a 45° angle) and cut them to length. Using a cutoff box like the one I'm using will help you make accurate crosscuts on wide panels.

STEP 3 After you've cut the profile at the bottom of the two back panels with a saber saw and ripped out and cut to length the two very narrow side panels (don't forget the 45° angle along one edge), take a few moments to do some careful layout of the locations of the dadoes. This is another of those very important first steps.

STEP 4 When the layout work has been completed, you're ready to cut the dadoes into which the cabinet top and bottom will be fastened. These can be cut on a table saw with a dado cutter or with a router equipped with a straight bit. They can also be cut with a dado plane, as shown here. If you're using a dado plane, clamp a batten adjacent to the planned dado. Then run the plane along the batten until the plane's depth stop bottoms out.

STEP 5 Before you fasten anything together, lay out the cabinet's four major pieces and study them to be sure everything will come together properly. Because of its unusual geometry, a corner cabinet presents some assembly challenges which are best solved by stopping from time to time to study the work in progress. Notice that all four of these components have been ripped with one edge at a 45° angle.

STEP 6 In order to align the cabinet's two back panels so that I could screw them together, I tightened one panel edge-up in my side vise and created a support for the lapping panel using a footstool and a couple of pieces of scrap material. I then turned in a line of 2" drywall screws. The array of drills is necessary for the different kinds of holes you need to drill at each location. The drill on the left is equipped with a countersink bit for the screw head. The two drills adjacent to that are fit with standard bits—one for the through hole in the lapping panel, the other for the threaded hole in the bottom panel.

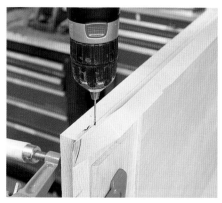

STEP 8 I fitted a ¼" plywood pattern before I cut out the top and bottom. (I later cut this pattern to the correct size for the three glass shelves and dropped it off at the glass shop.) I then screwed the top and bottom into their dadoes.

STEP 7 Before I could fasten the narrow cabinet sides to the back panels, I first created a kind of cradle for them by clamping a batten on the back of the cabinet back. The narrow cabinet side then slipped into the 45° slot. I tapped a few finish nails into some predrilled holes in the cabinet sides. I didn't intend for the finish nails to hold the cabinet sides permanently in place, only until I could screw them to the cabinet top and bottom and then glue two front pieces in place. The set-and-filled nail holes are a bit unsightly, but when the job is finished, they'll be tucked up tight against the wall.

STEP 9 The front of the cabinet is flush with the doors so I added a filler strip at the top of the cabinet (visible under the crown moulding), as well as the scroll below the doors. Each of these pieces is the same thickness as the doors and each is held in place with glue. Cut the miters for your mouldings on your table saw.

Moulding-making options

I have always made use of hand planes—to fine tune a tenon, to dress a panel too wide for my planer, to smooth a patch on a partially completed piece of casework—but since a bout of lymphoma, I have shifted from doing perhaps 20 to 25 percent of my shaping and smoothing with hand planes to doing 85 to 90 percent of this work with hand planes.

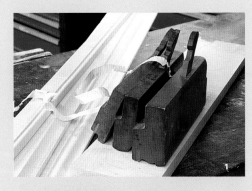

I set out on this new approach for reasons of health, but the switch from machine tools to hand tools has been beneficial in ways wholly unconnected to my health, introducing me to new and, in many instances, better ways of working.

Sticking mouldings in hard, figured maple with hand planes is hard work. (On the days I stuck mouldings, I passed on my afternoon walk.) But smoothing panels with a well-tuned infill plane is woodworking at its very best: rhythmic, soothing, satisfying and quiet. That's the most important thing. It's possible to think when you're working with a plane. I thought about was how much fun I was having with these planes on this material.

Nevertheless, you can form mouldings just as easily with a router as you can with moulding planes. That's the way I did it for many years.

Planning a Crown Moulding
I like to think of crown mouldings in three parts, each of which is formed from a separate piece of stock. The bottom element of the crown molding transitions down toward the cabinet. I used a Grecian ogee plane for this. Several ogee router bits could produce a similar effect. The next element, the one in the middle, I think of as the moulding's waist, and I frequently use a cove of some kind to create an appealing transition between the bottom and top elements of the moulding. For this particular crown molding, I used a No.7 round. For the top element in my moulding, I used a ³⁄₈" side bead. Here, too, it's possible to create a similar effect using a bead-cutting router bit.

The secret, I think, to creating attractive crown moldings is experimentation. Run a few inches of mouldings using each of your router bits. Then assemble them in different configurations until you get one that looks right. Remember that you can get a very different effect by cutting the moulding on the side of your stock rather than on the edge. Here, too, experimentation is important.

If you choose to create the crown molding using hand planes as I did, read on for some suggestions.

The first thing you must do is create smooth edges perpendicular to the faces of the boards you're moulding. With conventional material, this can be done quite nicely on a jointer. However, when you're working with figured material, sometimes even a well-tuned jointer can produce tearout. This is work for which a good plane—like the infill panel plane in **Photo 1**—is well suited.

In **Photo 2**, you can see the three elements of my crown moulding, as well as the three tools that created those elements.

Most complex molders (planes that produce a shape with more than one component) are sprung. That is, they are designed to work at an angle. The angle at which the plane is canted is indicated by a pair of crossed lines incised on the nose of the plane. One line representing vertical and the other representing horizontal **(Photo 3)**.

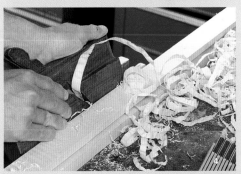

Rounds—like the one I used for my cove—don't have fences on their soles. They must be used against a batten (like the dado plane shown in step 4, page 153). In **photo 4**, I'm using a No. 7 round against a batten to create my cove.

The side bead is probably the easiest molding plane to master. It will quickly and efficiently cut a bead like the one you see in **Photo 5**. It needs no batten because its sole is equipped with a fence.

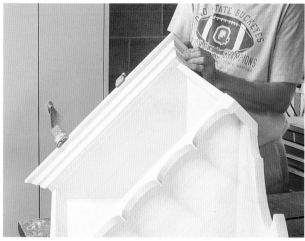

STEP 10 Use clamps to hold the large front section of the crown moulding in place while the glue dries. You can hand hold the two little ears of molding on either side for about 30 seconds until the glue sets.

STEP 11 Drill the shelf bracket holes.

STEP 12 Mill the door frames to the final thickness and width. Then, on the front of each piece, cut a bead with a ¼" side-bead plane. This is a smaller version of the ⅜" side bead I used on the top element of the cabinet's crown moulding. See "moulding-making options".

STEP 13 On the back side of the door frame stock, cut a rabbet using a plane called a moving filletster. You can also make the rabbets using a dado cutter on the table saw or using a straight bit in a router.

STEP 14 Cut the miters on the table saw and clean them up using a plane and a shooting board.

STEP 15 Cut the notches for the feathers that hold the doors together. Then resaw the feather stock and plane it to nearly the exact thickness (it must be just a tad thinner in order to slide into the notches slathered with glue). Then mark and cut the feather stock to fit each of the notches.

STEP 16 The grain in the feather must run perpendicular to the miter joint it is crossing. If the grain runs parallel to the miter, the feather won't have any strength.

STEP 17 Make a clamping table to apply pressure to all four sides of the doors while the glued feathers cured. The table is a plywood surface with screwed blocks, each of which is a bit outside the limits of the door frame. Cut pairs of wedges to fit inside each of the blocks. By tapping the paired wedges together, pressure is applied to all sides of the door while holding it squarely. (As an option, you can reinforce the joinery with flat brass corners screwed to the back side of the doors.)

STEP 18 Mark and cut each of the door hinge mortises.

STEP 19 Define the outline of the mortise and cut the sides to depth using a chisel.

STEP 20 Clean out the mortise using a chisel.

STEP 21 Many years ago, I discovered the center punch and in an instant, my hinge installation improved dramatically. With this tool, you don't have to guess at the center of every screw hole on a hinge. The center punch finds the center, then punches a shallow depression that you can use to register the tip of your drill bit. In the photo at left, you can see the tapered tip of the center punch protruding through a screw hole in a hinge leaf. Because that tip is tapered, it automatically locates the center of the hole. In the photo at right, I'm using the punch to mark holes.

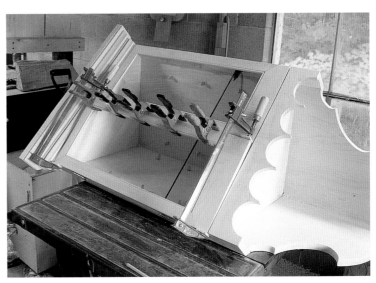

STEP 22 After you've installed the hinges on the doors, hold each door in place while you mark the location of the hinge mortises on the cabinet sides. Remove the hinges from the door. Holding each hinge in position on the cabinet side, mark around the hinge, then cut the mortises and install the hinges just as you did on the door frames.

STEP 23 Finally, add a little bead between the doors, recessing it just a bit. This detail, which I stole from many period originals, adds an appealing visual accent.

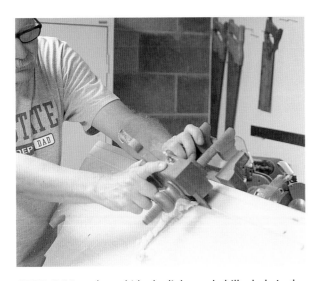

STEP 24 In order to hide the light cord, drill a hole in the cabinet top and another hole in the cabinet back. Then, on the back side of the cabinet back, plow a groove that intersects the drilled hole in the cabinet back. I cut this groove with a plow plane, but you might choose to cut it with a router and a straight bit.

After the cabinet is finished, mount the light, cut the plug from the light cord, feed the cord through the hole in the cabinet top, the hole in the cabinet back, and lay the cord in the plowed groove. The groove allows the cord to exit the cabinet at the very bottom. Then put a new plug on the cord

STEP 25 Apply two coats of rub-on finish and fasten the glass door panels in place with a thin bead of clear silicone in the rabbets on the back of the door frame. Install the doors and the door hardware. Hang the cabinet from a pair of lag bolts that pass through holes in the tops of the two cabinet backs (these holes are hidden by the crown molding) and penetrate a pair of wall studs.

QUEEN ANNE SIDE TABLES

Build these traditional tables with help
from a tool usually reserved for carpenters:
the power planer.

by Jim Stuard

As I get a little older, I get more sedentary. My wife says I'm just looking for more places to set a drink down. In that spirit, I decided to draw on my experience making period furniture to come up with a set of end tables for the living room — one with a poplar clover-shaped top, the other with a curly maple porringer top. These tables come from designs that are roughly 250 years old. This places them squarely in the country interpretation of the Queen Anne style.

According to Leigh Keno, a noted New York antiques dealer and a regular on PBS's popular Antiques Roadshow, the term porringer is merely a convenient way for antique dealers to classify this type of table and probably has nothing to do with the way the table was used originally. Using the English word porridge (oatmeal) as the root word, the term is likely no more than 150 years old. Porringer is used today to describe a small soup or cereal bowl with a handle. Antique dealers most likely tried to use the name to pass off the round oversized corners — which were no more than a decorative element — as the accessories of a small breakfast table. That said, porringers in good condition will fetch thousands of dollars these days due to their rarity.

Making Aprons

These tables were made with simple mortise-and-tenon construction. Start by cutting the apron parts according to the Schedule of Materials. Next cut the ⅜" by 4"-wide by ⅞"-long tenons on the ends of the aprons.

Making Pockets

The last thing to do on the aprons is to drill the pocket holes for attaching the base to the top. Do this on a drill press with a 1¼" Forstner bit. Use a shop-built jig (the diagram for this jig is on page 164) to hold the aprons in place for drilling.

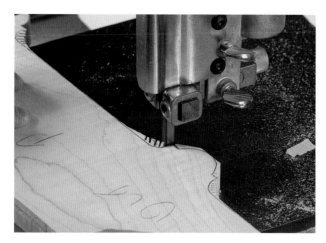

STEP 1 Lay out the scrollwork on the bottom of the aprons using the patterns supplied on page 164. Glue the patterns to ¼" plywood, cut them out, trace the pattern on your aprons and cut them out on a band saw. Make relief cuts on the inside radii so you can scroll them out easier.

STEP 2 When drilling pocket holes, make sure that the bottom of the pocket is at least ⅞" from the top edge of the apron to prevent the screws from poking through.

Leg Blanks

Although the legs look complicated, they are not. The secret is an offset turning technique. First cut the blanks ⅛" longer than in the schedule. This gives you some room to work with when turning the pad on the end of the foot.

Use a straightedge to make an X from corner to corner on both ends of the blank. This will aid in finding the center as well as marking the offset. Now, on the bottom of the legs, determine which corner will face out. On the bottom of each leg, measure ½" from the center to the corner opposite the outside corner. This is the offset for the leg. Remember, the farther away from the center you go, the thinner the ankle (the area just above the pad) will be. Going any farther than ½" is dangerously close to having a leg pop off your lathe.

Mark a line completely around the blank 6" down from the top of the blank. To save time roughing the blank, lay out a 1½"-diameter circle on the bottom of the blank. Set your jointer to 45°. Using the circle as a guide, lower the infeed table to the point where you can take the corner off, leaving about ¹⁄₃₂" to the circle. Go slow and joint to within ⅛" of the line where the turning starts. Now mount the blank in the lathe.

After mounting a blank between centers with the top toward the drive center, cut a small kerf at the line where the turning stops. Don't cut too far or you won't be able to remove the kerf. With a roughing gouge and a skew chisel, turn a cylindrical blank from the saw kerf to the foot. At this point use a skew chisel to

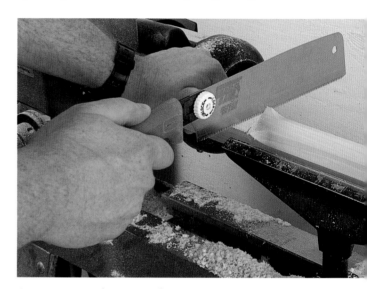

STEP 3 To cut the corners, first mount a blank between centers with the top toward the drive center. Then use a saw to cut a small kerf on each corner at the line 6" from the top. Don't cut too far or you won't be able to remove the kerf. With a roughing gouge and a skew chisel, turn a cylindrical blank from the saw kerf to the foot. At this point use a skew chisel to cut a small rounding up on the square corners of the top (see diagram). Repeat on all the legs and you're ready to do the offset turning.

round the corners of the pummel, the square part of the leg, where it meets the turned portion. Repeat on all the legs and you're ready to do the offset turning.

Turning the Offset

Before resetting the legs, measure up from the bottom ⅛" and from that mark another ⅝". Turn the lathe on and follow the marks around with a pencil. Take a parting tool and set it on its side. Cut a small inci-

sion at the ⅝" mark. This creates a shadow line from which to begin the offset turning. Set the lathe for its lowest speed and reset the tailstock so the leg center is mounted in the offset mark. This might look like an awkward setup, but as you remove material the leg will turn with more stability. Finish the straight part of the leg with a skew chisel and the ankle with a roughing gouge. Finally, turn the pad foot as shown in step 5. Now is the time to sand the legs. Start with 120-grit sandpaper and finish with 150 grit.

Now cut the ⅜" × ⅞" × 4" mortises in the legs, ⁵⁄₁₆" in from the edge and ½" down from the top. Be careful when marking the locations of your mortises to make sure the turned feet face out. You'll notice that the mortises meet slightly at their bottoms. Simply plane away a little of the tenon where they meet. Now glue the base together. Start by gluing the short ends together and then attaching them to the long aprons.

After the glue is dry, finish sand the entire base, then lay out the holes for the cherry pegs. Any dark hardwood will do for the pegs, but cherry sands smooth and the end grain stains a dark color. Drill a ¼" hole 1" deep. Follow suit with ³⁄₁₆" and ⅛" bits, creating a tapered hole. After shaping 16 square pegs (tapered on four sides to a point), tap one in until you feel and hear it seat. The sound of the hammer hitting the peg makes a distinctly different sound when it seats. No glue is required for this as you are running a peg completely through the leg. It won't be

coming out anytime soon. Cut the pegs, leaving ¹⁄₃₂" showing and sand until it is a rounded-over bump. Drill ¼" holes into the pockets from the top of the base for attaching the top.

Make and Attach the Top

The top is the easiest part, but it can make or break the whole project. Wood selection is key. One hundred years ago, you could get extremely wide, highly figured curly maple at a low price. Amazingly most old porringers were one- or two-board tops. That's clear-figured wood 10" to 20" wide! Regrettably, those days are gone, and you will have to make do with the painfully high priced, narrow lumber you get today.

Poplar is easy to get in a decent width and length, but I had to try the Amish sawmills in eastern Pennsylvania to find a retail source for decent curly maple. I managed to find decent 4/4 that's about 7" wide and a nice piece of 8/4 for the legs. I wasn't sure how thick

STEP 4 When you turn the lathe on, the leg's spinning creates a ghost image of what the finished leg will look like. Remove that "ghost" material with a roughing gouge. Stop at the second line that you drew earlier. Lay the gouge on its left side at the second line and slowly rotate the gouge clockwise as you go to the left. Go very slowly until you get the hang of how the wood reacts to the gouge.

STEP 5 The last thing to do on the legs is turning the pad on the foot. You do this last, as removing the foot material also removes the offset center. Reset the bottom of the leg into the original center and, using a parting tool, turn away this "extra" length until it's about ³⁄₈" diameter. This gives you some extra distance from the live center. Then using a small spindle gouge, turn the pad of the foot till it meets the ³⁄₈" diameter. Sand the pad the same as the leg and you're done turning.

STEP 6 When you've done all you can with a power planer, use chisels and planes to sculpt underneath and remove material down to the marked line.

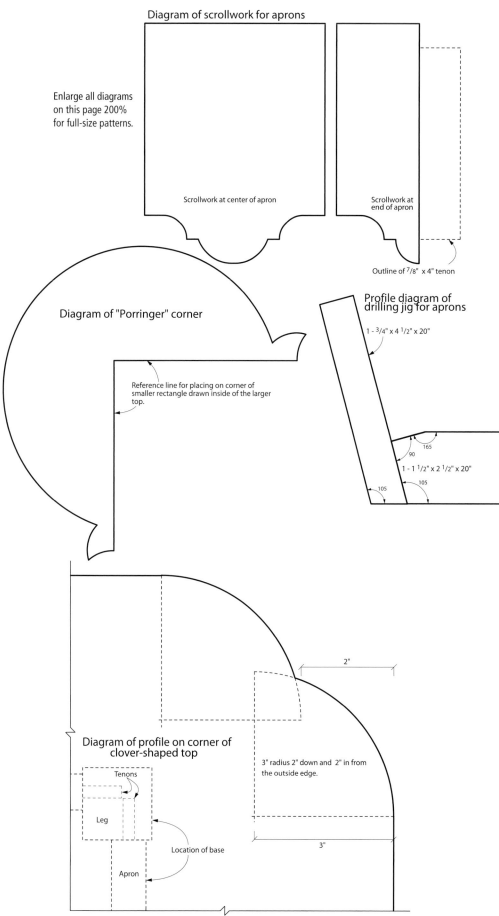

Diagram of scrollwork for aprons

Enlarge all diagrams
on this page 200%
for full-size patterns.

Scrollwork at center of apron

Scrollwork at
end of apron

Outline of $7/8$" x 4" tenon

Diagram of "Porringer" corner

Reference line for placing on corner of
smaller rectangle drawn inside of the larger
top.

Profile diagram of
drilling jig for aprons

1 - 3/4" x 4 1/2" x 20"

165
90
105   105
1 - 1 1/2" x 2 1/2" x 20"

2"

3" radius 2" down and 2" in from
the outside edge.

3"

Diagram of profile on corner of
clover-shaped top

Tenons

Leg

Location of base

Apron

the legs would be when
I started, so you could
probably get away with
6/4 for leg stock.

The tops for both
types of tables are the
same size. They just re-
quire a different edge
pattern. See diagram
at left for the shape of
each top. For the por-
ringer top, lay out a
15¼" x 25⅛" rectangle
in the center of the top.
Make a pattern for the
top with ¼" plywood as
you did with the aprons.
When you lay the inside
corner of the pattern
over the outside corner
of the drawn rectangle,
the outside of the radius
should just touch the
edge of the top. Trace
the pattern on all four
corners and jigsaw the
top out. For the clover-
shaped top, things are
easier. Make a pattern
from the diagram sup-
plied at left and trace the
double radius on all four
corners.

When you are done
cutting out the shape
of the top, chamfer the
edges. Chamfering the
edges lightens the overall
look of the table, and the
chisel work underneath
has a very sculptural feel.
Before chamfering, use a
marking gauge to mark a
line that is half the thickness of the top on the
entire outside edge of
the top. Next, use an ad-
justable square to mark a

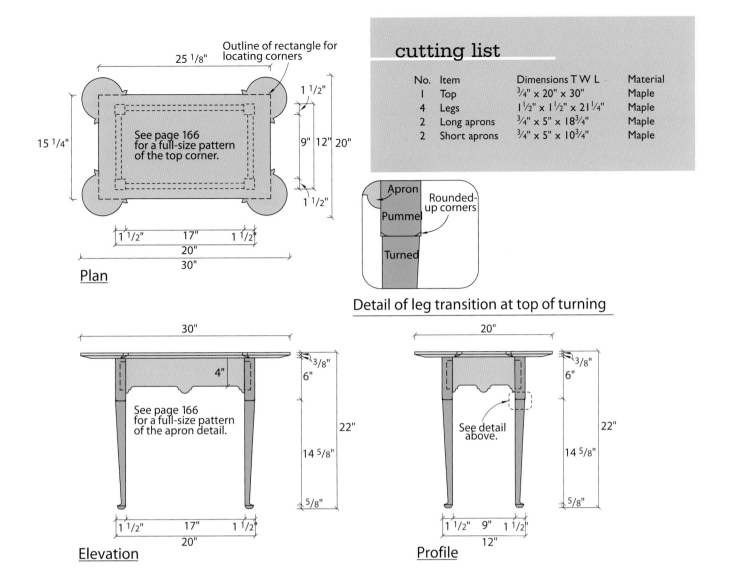

cutting list

No.	Item	Dimensions T W L	Material
1	Top	¾" x 20" x 30"	Maple
4	Legs	1½" x 1½" x 21¼"	Maple
2	Long aprons	¾" x 5" x 18¾"	Maple
2	Short aprons	¾" x 5" x 10¾"	Maple

Plan

Detail of leg transition at top of turning

Elevation

Profile

line around the underside of the top. For the porringer the measurement is 1½" and for the clover use a 2¼" line.

I chamfered the edges with a power planer. It's a tool used mostly by carpenters to remove material from doors when fitting and installing them. And in that role, this tool is unequaled. Finish sand the top to 150 grit.

The last assembly chore is to screw the top to the base. Begin by laying the top upside down on a blanket. Center the base on the top and screw it down with no. 10 × 1½" wood screws.

In finishing the clover table, I sprayed on a custom-mixed aniline dye followed by three coats of clear finish. This turned the poplar to a mahogany-like color.

The porringer was a different story. To begin finishing, I hand-scraped the top with a Stanley #80 cabinet scraper. With the lack of abrasive sandpaper 250 years ago, this is how the old tables were made ready to fin-

How Thick Is It Anyway?

When lumberyards count up the board footage that you buy, it's referred to as a tally. The "tallyman" carries a special notebook and a strange floppy stick called a "tallystick" (go figure!) with odd measurements on it. The lumber you buy is sorted by how many quarters of an inch thick it is. This system starts at 4/4 for 1" thickness on up to 16/4 for 4" lumber.

ish. Scraping with a properly prepared scraper blade will show up as rows of slight depressions ($\frac{1}{32}$" deep) with ridges about 2½" apart. I stained the wood with aniline dye, then applied one coat of boiled linseed oil and finished the table with four coats of dark shellac. This imparts a nice honey brown color to the curly maple and is easy to repair. Now where did I put that drink?

Shaker Tall Clock

Brother Benjamin Youngs' clock is an exquisite example of how a simple Shaker design can carry across the ages, and still have a foot firmly planted in two centuries.

by Steve Shanesy

You'd never guess what the most inspiring aspect of building this clock was. Not the awesome curly maple or rich-looking finish, but something altogether plain – the clock's paper face.

Nice, but what's so special about it, you ask? It was hand-drawn and lettered using 100-year-old drawing instruments passed down from my great-grandfather, a draftsman, who laid out track beds for the railroads. The set, made in Manchester, England, by A. G. Thornton & Co., and lovingly stored in a velvet- and satin-lined walnut box, contains calipers, two delicately turned ivory handled inkers, and finely tooled and incredibly machined compasses.

After experimenting with these special tools I was ready to put pen to parchment. As I did so I was amazed at the tool's ability to guide the drawing tip, rendering the precise lines. In making my clock face I imagined for a brief moment looking over my great-grandfather's shoulder as he sat at his drawing board.

Using this old way of drawing was infinitely more simple to figure out than assembling the various parts that made up the clock's works. Most parts were obvious as to their function: the works, pendulum, weights, chain, etc. But how they mounted, attached or were oriented to each other was a complete mystery. They arrived in a kit without the first hint of instruction, and left me scratching my head. Thank goodness building the clock's case was easier than figuring out the works. Easier, because I had the help of three books referencing this famous clock made by Brother Benjamin, so determining overall dimensions was relatively easy, save for the fact none of them agreed exactly.

Lower Case

The original Shaker clock was built from poplar, but I had just enough curly maple to do the job. One board was even wide

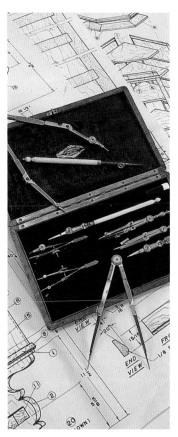

These are my great-grandfather's drawing instruments, which I used to hand letter the clock's face.

Upper Case

The upper case that shrouds the clock's works uses the same joints for the back and top as in the lower case. A ⅜"-thick rail is haunch-tenoned and mortised into the sides at the bottom of the front to hold the sides square and in place. When glued up and still in the clamps, pin the tenons using ³⁄₁₆" dowel stock. After the upper case is assembled, add a filler strip to the front upper edge that's as long as the front is wide and ¾" square. This build-up accommodates the thickness of the door so that the top chamfered moulding is correctly positioned.

The upper door has a cockbead detail on its outside edge. To create the detail, take 10 minutes to make a simple scratch stock using a flat-head screw. Simply insert the screw in the end of a block that fits comfortably in your hand. Let the head project out about ¼". With a hacksaw, cut the projecting screw head in half from top to bottom. Dress the cutting edge (the face) with a file, and use a small triangular file to relieve the back.

enough to make the 12"-wide front, which is where I began construction. To keep the look of a single-board front, cut the board to length then rip from each edge the "stiles" at the door opening. Next, cut out the door opening 30" up from the bottom, then 9" from the top. When done, mark the orientation of the pieces. Now glue the front together again, less the opening for the door.

Next, cut a ½" x ¾" rabbet along the inside back edge and top edge of the two side pieces. Mill the same rabbet on the top of the front piece, and on the back edge of the top as well. While working on the top, also make the cutout to accommodate the swinging pendulum and the hanging chains from the works (see diagram). The front and sides are then glued up using a simple butt joint to take advantage of the long-grain to long-grain connection, while the top is glued and nailed in place. Before screwing in the back, fasten cleats to the front and sides (20" up from the bottom edge) to be used later to attach the bottom panel.

When the case is complete, make the two-part base using a ½"-radius profile bit for the wider piece and ¼" for the smaller base shoe. Miter the front corners and cut a rabbet on the other end for the base back. The front and sides of the base sleeve over the lower case about 1" and are fastened from the inside of the case.

The homemade 10-minute cockbeading tool in use.

These 90° clamps made gluing up the top case a lot easier. Getting things square was a real snap.

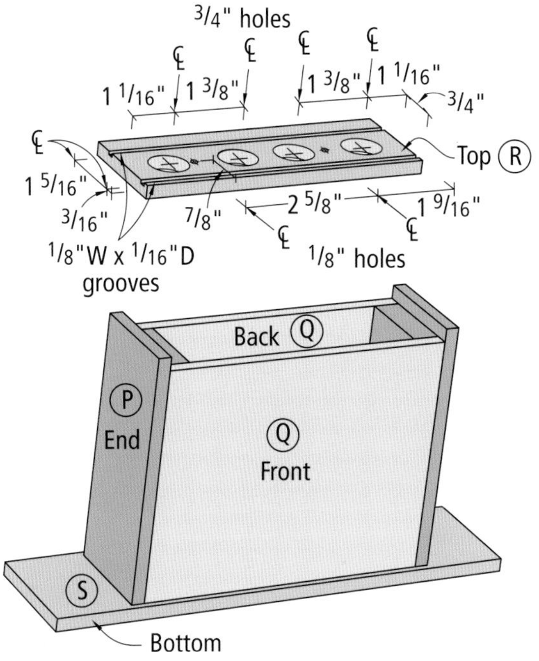

Detail of hole locations in riser box

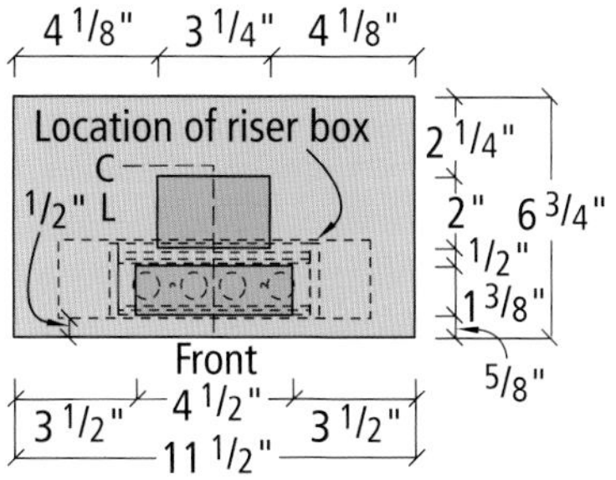

Detail of case top cutouts

SUPPLIES

Klockit
800-556-2548 or klockit.com
1 • Hermle movement #1161-853

cutting list

	NO.	LET.	ITEM	T	W	L	MATERIAL
Lower case							
❑	1	A	Front	3/4	12	65	P
❑	1	B	Door	3/4	6 7/8	25 7/8	P
❑	2	C	Sides	3/4	6 1/4	65	P
❑	1	D	Back	3/4	11 1/2	64 3/4	PL
❑	1	E	Top	3/4	6 3/4	11 1/2	PL
❑	1	F	Bottom	3/4	5 1/2	11 1/2	PL
Upper case							
❑	2	G	Sides	3/4	7 1/2	15	P
❑	1	H	Back	3/4	14	14 3/4	P
❑	1	I	Top	3/4	7 1/2	14	PL
❑	1	J	Front rail	3/8	1 1/4	13 3/4	P
❑	2	K	Door stiles	3/4	2	14 3/16	P
❑	2	L	Door rails	3/4	2	14 9/16	P
❑	1	M	Face panel	1/4	13	12 13/16	H
❑	1	N	Face cover		13	12 13/16	C
❑	1	O	Buildup	3/4	3/4	14 1/2	P
Clockworks stand							
❑	2	P	Ends	3/4	2	4 3/16	S
❑	2	Q	Front/back	1/4	4 7/16	5 1/2	PL
❑	1	R	Top	1/4	2	5 1/2	PL
❑	1	S	Bottom	1/4	2 3/8	9	PL

(DIMENSIONS (INCHES): T, W, L)

Mouldings

Top chamfer: 36" of 3/4" sq.
Cove: 36" of 2 1/8" sq.
Base: 36" of 3/4" x 3 1/2"
Base shoe: 1/2" x 1"

P=primary wood, maple; PL= plywood; S=secondary wood, poplar; H=hardboard; C=copper

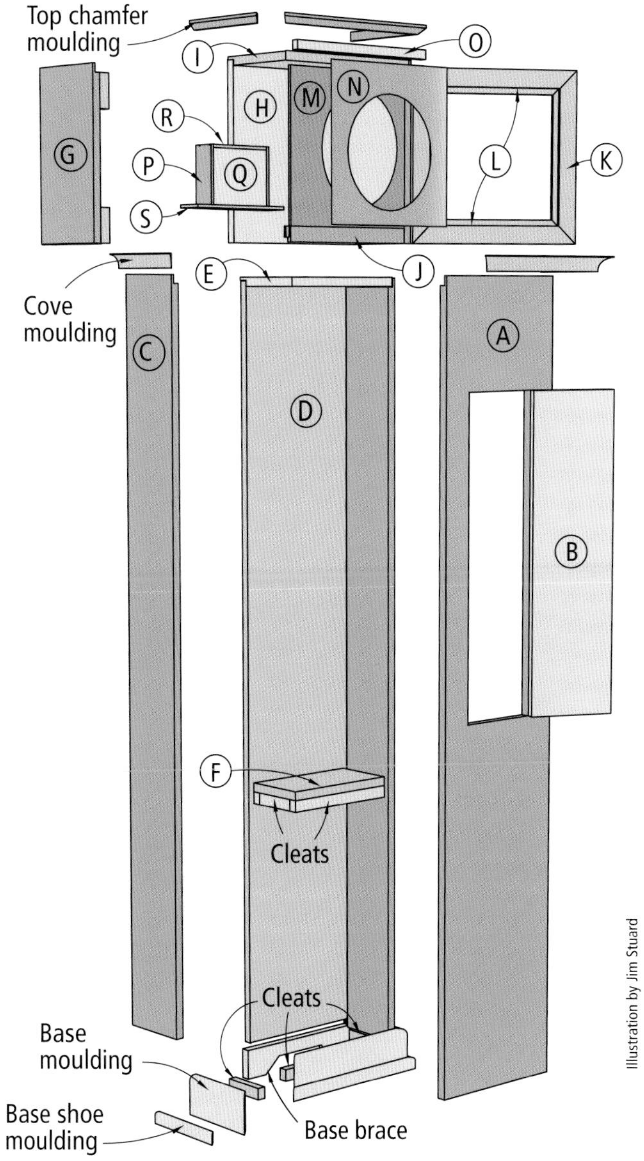

Exploded view

Illustration by Jim Stuard

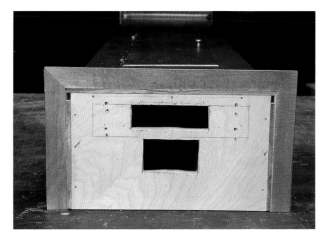

Cut the cockbead on the milled stock for the door frame, then cut a ½"-square rabbet on the back inside edge of the stock to let in the glass. Now cut the parts to length and glue up.

Now, make the last mouldings you'll need. The chamfer at the top is easy. Run it, miter the corners and judiciously nail it in place. I used only a dab of polyurethane glue at the center of the moulding because its grain runs contrary to that of the sides.

The cove moulding is more difficult to produce and is made from a triangular-shaped length of wood using the table saw. By clamping an auxiliary fence at a severe, oblique angle to the blade, the part is then run with the blade just above the table, raising it slightly after each pass. Thank goodness only about three linear feet are required because this method requires a lot of sanding to remove the mill marks from the blade. When finished sanding, cut the miters and attach it just like the chamfer moulding.

You may be wondering how the top case attaches to the lower. It doesn't. It simply rests on top and lifts off to access the works (after removing the hands).

I'm sure Brother Youngs did not use copper sheet metal to surround the face outside the clock face proper, but I did. I made the round cutout using a router mounted on a circle-cutting jig. It's a very simple process. When done, I used a random-orbit sander and 220-grit paper to put a satin-like sheen on the copper, followed by a coat of shellac to retard tarnishing. The hardboard and copper are mounted inside the upper case on cleats positioned to coincide with the mounting location of the works (see diagram).

The last bit of building is the small box on which the works sit. Its height is especially critical because that determines the height at which the stem protrudes through the hole in the face. Make the box using ¾"-solid poplar sides and ¼" Baltic birch top and bottom. Note that the bottom is wider and longer. Use the extra length to screw it down. Follow the diagram to position the holes in the top of the box where the chains run through.

Before the upper door can be hung, install the glass. I used glass from stock I salvaged from old houses. This old material has imperfections in the thickness which cause ever-so-slight distortions and adds to the authentic look of the piece. Regardless of the glass you use, install it using glazing points and glazing compound.

Now the upper door is ready to hang. The hinges in the clock kit don't require mortising so attach them directly. The lower door is the same. However, before hanging the door, run a ¼"-radius profile on the outside edges. Then attach the hinges to allow it to set ¼" proud of the case.

It goes without saying that I was just itching to set

Clock Face

I used the clock face from the clock works package as a guide to lay out my paper face. Construction need not change if you use the painted aluminum face in the kit. In either case, fix the clock face to ¼" tempered hardboard using spray adhesive. Then drill a ⁵⁄₁₆" hole in the center of the face.

It's simple work to ink the lines for the paper face. After you make the three circles, use a compass to ink the top and bottom of the Roman numerals (right). Then ink the straight lines to fill in the numerals. It's not calligraphy, so you don't have to worry about curving lines far right).

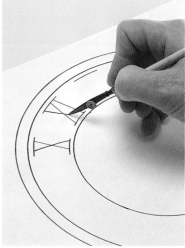

up the works and check everything out. It's a good idea to do this before sanding and finishing anyway. Set it up and let it run overnight.

Final Touches

Thoroughly sand all the surfaces starting with 100 grit and progress up to 180 using a random-orbit sander. Break all the edges by hand with 120 grit. After removing the dust, color the wood using water-based aniline dye called Golden Amber Maple made by J.E. Moser (available through Woodworker's Supply, 800-645-9292 or woodworker.com). Because the water raises the grain, very carefully and lightly hand sand the flat surfaces with 360-grit paper. Be extremely cautious near edges. Don't sand through the color. Dust again, then apply a light coat of boiled linseed oil. As a penetrating finish, this step plays an important factor in making the curly figure on the wood pop. When done, rub down with a clean rag to remove any excess oil. Wait 24 hours to allow the oil to dry, then brush on four coats of amber shellac in a two-pound cut. Lightly sand between coats.

The unusual experiences of learning how to set up a mechanical-works clock along with creating the clock face from my heirloom drawing set added a new dimension to the satisfaction I always find at the conclusion of a project. I felt in touch with a distant branch of my family tree, rather than merely reproducing an artifact from the past. Some day, should my tall clock find its way into one of my children's homes, I hope my name, scrawled on the clock face, will imbue a similar sentiment.

Horology 101

I didn't know what "horology" meant when I received the big box full of clock parts for this project. Fortunately, I had a dictionary, so I quickly learned it means "the art of making time pieces." Too bad there wasn't a reference for identifying and assembling the clock parts. I'm still a long way from being an expert, but for this project at least, I think I can talk you through.

The "works" are the gears and movements that are sandwiched between a front and back plate. The works for this project are made by Hermle (see Supplies box). They are weight-driven, require resetting the chains every eight days, strike a bell once on the half hour and ring the hour with the number of rings for the hour struck.

The works have the stem for the hands facing front, of course, and the pendulum faces rear. The pendulum attaches to the works with a narrow, metal part called a leader.

The works require two weights suspended on two chains. One weight drives the time-keeping job of the works, the other provides the energy to make the chimes work. The weights use equal lengths of chain and so are reset at the same time.

When facing the works, the chains go over the sprockets with the weights on the outside of each sprocket. (When you set the chains on the sprockets make sure they are not twisted and are seated properly.) The weights are attached to the chains with an "S" hook.

Each lead weight goes inside a brass tube called a shell. Each tube has two end caps with holes where a rod with threaded ends go through, which keeps the whole thing together, with a nut on the bottom and hook on the top.

The hands of the clock fit on the stem, which consists of two parts, one inside the other. The hour hand goes on first and sleeves over the outside part of the stem. It is a tight press fit slipped on in the appropriate direction of the given hour. The minute hand, on the other hand (sorry!), has a square bushing and sleeves onto the inner

part of the stem. It must be adjusted by turning the bushing that's pressed into the hand. A decorative brass nut holds the minute hand in place.

The pendulum helps regulate the speed of the clock. If it's running fast, you adjust the brass-colored circle down, making the travel of the swing longer. Moving it up shortens the travel, making the clock faster if it's running slow.

The beat of the clock – that's the rhythm of the tick/tock sound, is also important. Like your heart, it wants to be regular. Tap your finger to each tick/tock sound. The time between taps should be equal. Adjust the beat by moving the escapement ever so slightly. The escapement is the "C" shaped metal part in the center upper back of the works. It regulates the gear that's connected by a rod to the top of the leader from which the pendulum hangs.

The works are attached to the top of the box on which it mounts using two long, thin machine screws. They thread into tapped holes in the lower bars, which hold the front and back metal plates of the works together.

The works are mounted to a plywood box that rests   on the lower case.

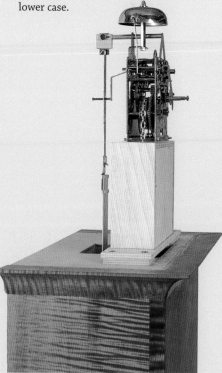

Read This Import ant Safety Notice

To prevent accidents, keep safety in mind while you work. Use the safety guards installed on power equipment; they are for your protection.

When working on power equipment, keep fingers away from saw blades, wear safety goggles to prevent injuries from flying wood chips and sawdust, wear hearing protection and consider installing a dust vacuum to reduce the amount of airborne sawdust in your woodshop.

Don't wear loose clothing, such as neckties or shirts with loose sleeves, or jewelry, such as rings, necklaces or bracelets, when working on power equipment. Tie back long hair to prevent it from getting caught in your equipment.

People who are sensitive to certain chemicals should check the chemical content of any product before using it. Due to the variability of local conditions, construction materials, skill levels, etc., neither the author nor Popular Woodworking Books assumes any responsibility for any accidents, injuries, damages or other losses incurred resulting from the material presented in this book.

The authors and editors who compiled this book have tried to make the contents as accurate and correct as possible. Plans, illustrations, photographs and text have been carefully checked. All instructions, plans and projects should be carefully read, studied and understood before beginning construction.

Prices listed for supplies and equipment were current at the time of publication and are subject to change.

Traditional Country Furniture. Copyright © 2013 by F+W Media, Inc. Printed and bound in China. All rights reserved. No part of this book may be reproduced in any form or by any electronic or mechanical means including information storage and retrieval systems without permission in writing from the publisher, except by a reviewer, who may quote brief passages in a review. Published by Popular Woodworking Books, an imprint of F+W Media, Inc., 10151 Carver Rd., Suite 200, Blue Ash, Ohio, 45242. (800) 289-0963 First edition.

Distributed in Canada by Fraser Direct
100 Armstrong Avenue
Georgetown, Ontario L7G 5S4
Canada

Distributed in the U.K. and Europe by
F&W Media International, LTD
Brunel House, Forde Close
Newton Abbot
TQ12 4PU, UK
Tel: (+44) 1626 323200
Fax: (+44) 1626 323319
E-mail: enquiries@fwmedia.com

Distributed in Australia by Capricorn Link
P.O. Box 704
Windsor, NSW 2756
Australia
Tel: (+02) 4560 1600
Fax: (+02) 4577 5288
E-mail: books@capricornlink.com.au

Visit our website at www.popularwoodworking.com or our consumer website at www.shopwoodworking.com for more woodworking information projects. Other fine Popular Woodworking Books are available from your local bookstore or direct from the publisher.

17 16 15 14 13   5 4 3 2 1

Acquisitions editor: David Thiel
Designer: Geoff Raker
Production coordinator: Debbie Thomas

METRIC CONVERSION CHART

to convert	to	multiply by
Inches	Centimeters	2.54
Centimeters	Inches	0.4
Feet	Centimeters	30.5
Centimeters	Feet	0.03
Yards	Meters	0.9
Meters	Yards	1.1

Resources

Ball and Ball
463 West Lincoln Hwy.
Exton, PA 19341
(800) 257-3711
www.ballandball.com
Antique hardware reproductions and restoration

Highland Woodworking
1045 North Highland Ave. NE
Atlanta, GA 30306
(800) 241-6748
www.highlandwoodworking.com
Tools, woodworking supplies, books

Horton Brasses, Inc.
49 Nooks Hill Rd.
Cromwell, CT 06416
(800) 754-9127
www.horton-brasses.com
Fine reproduction brass and iron hardware

Klingspor Abrasives, Inc.
2555 State Blvd. SE
Hickory, NC 28602
(800) 645-5555
www.klingspor.com
Sandpaper of all kinds

Klockit
N3211 County Road H
Lake Geneva, WI 53147
(800) 556-2548
www.klockit.com
Parts and kits for clocks, small and large

Lee Valley Tools, Ltd.
P.O Box 1780
Ogdensburg, NY 13669-6780
(800) 871-8158
www.leevalley.com
Woodworking tools and hardware

Merit Industries
1020 North 10th Street
Kansas City, KS 66101 (800) 856-4441
www.meritindustries.com
Finishing supplies

Rockler
4365 Willow Dr.
Medina, MN 55340
(800) 279-4441
www.rockler.com
Woodworking tools, hardware and books

Van Dyke's Restorers
P.O. Box 52
Louisiana, MO 63353
(800) 558-1234
www.vandykes.com
Antique hardware reproductions and restoration

Woodcraft Supply
1177 Rosemar Rd.
P.O. Box 1686
Parkersburg, WV 26102
(800) 225-1153
www.woodcraft.com
Woodworking supplies, hardware, tools and books

Woodworker's Supply
1108 N. Glenn Rd.
Casper, WY 82601
(800) 645-9292
www.woodworker.com
Woodworking tools and accessories, finishing supplies books and plans

Ideas. Instruction. Inspiration.

These and other great Popular Woodworking products are available at your local bookstore, woodworking store or online supplier.

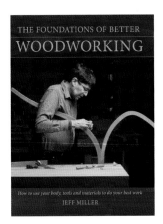

THE FOUNDATIONS OF BETTER WOODWORKING
By Jeff Miller

The secret to producing beautiful furniture that you and your family will treasure for generations starts with the fundamentals – those essential, yet often overlooked principles upon which all of your skills should be based. You'll learn to use your body, tools and materials to do your best work.

hardcover · 192 pages

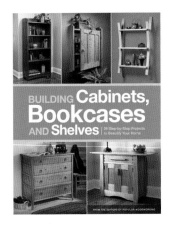

BUILDING CABINETS, BOOKCASES AND SHELVES

Whether you need storage for books, DVDs, games or clothes, you'll find attractive, custom options in this book.With 29 storage solutions in a variety of styles and sizes, each project includes cutting lists and step-by-step instructions from professional woodworkers.

paperback · 208 pages

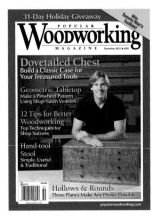

POPULAR WOODWORKING MAGAZINE

Whether learning a new hobby or perfecting your craft, *Popular Woodworking Magazine* provides seven issues a year with the expert information you need to learn the skills, not just build the project. Find the latest issue on newsstands, or you can order online at popularwoodworking.com.

SUPER-TUNE A HANDPLANE
By Christopher Schwarz

Whether your plane is old or new, discover tips that will make it perform with surgical precision. With just a little effort and a couple hours, you can super tune any handplane into a high-performance tool.

 Available at shopwoodworking.com DVD & Instant download

POPULAR WOODWORKING'S VIP PROGRAM
Get the Most Out of Woodworking!

Join the ShopWoodworking VIP program today for the tools you need to advance your woodworking abilities. Your one-year paid renewal membership includes:

· *Popular Woodworking Magazine* (1 year/7 issue U.S. subscription — a $21.97 value)

· *Popular Woodworking Magazine* CD — Get all issues of *Popular Woodworking Magazine* from 2006 to to 2010 (a $64.95 value!)

· *The Best of Shops & Workbenches* CD — 62 articles on workbenches, shop furniture, shop organization and essential jigs and fixtures (a $15 value)

· Roubo Plate 11 Poster — A beautiful 18" x 24" reproduction of Plate 11 from Andre Roubo's 18th-century masterpiece *L'Art du Menuisier*, on heavy, cream-colored stock

· 20% Members-Only Savings on 6-Month Subscription for ShopClass OnDemand

· 10% Members-Only Savings at Shopwoodworking.com

· 10% Members-Only Savings on FULL PRICE Registration for Woodworking In America Conference (Does Not Apply with Early Bird Price)

· and more....

Visit **popularwoodworking.com** to see more woodworking information by the experts, learn about our digital subscription and sign up to receive our weekly newsletter at popularwoodworking.com/newsletters/
